Sharing and Responding

Third Edition

Peter Elbow
University of Massachusetts at Amherst

Pat Belanoff
State University of New York at Stony Brook

McGraw Hill

Boston   Burr Ridge, IL   Dubuque, IA   Madison, WI   New York   San Francisco   St. Louis
Bangkok   Bogotá   Caracas   Lisbon   London   Madrid
Mexico City   Milan   New Delhi   Seoul   Singapore   Sydney   Taipei   Toronto

Our cover image depicts a traditional *mola,* a colorful, intricately appliquéd fabric panel created by the Kuna Indians, a tribal society living on a chain of islands off of Panama's Caribbean coast.

McGraw-Hill Higher Education

A Division of The **McGraw-Hill** *Companies*

SHARING AND RESPONDING

This book is printed on acid-free paper.

2 3 4 5 6 7 8 9 0 DOC/DOC   0 9 8 7 6 5 4 3 2 1 0

ISBN 0–07–303179–8

Editorial director: *Phillip A. Butcher*
Senior sponsoring editor: *Lisa Moore*
Developmental editor II: *Alexis Walker*
Marketing manager: *Thayne Conrad*
Project manager: *Susanne Riedell*
Manager, new book production: *Melonie Salvati*
Senior designer: *Jennifer McQueen Hollingsworth*
Interior designer: *Maureen McCutcheon*
Cover photo: *Copyright 1999 PhotoDisc, Inc. All rights reserved.*
Photo researcher: *Judy Kausal*
Senior supplement coordinator: *Marc Mattson*
Compositor: *ElectraGraphics, Inc.*
Typeface: *10/12 Caslon 224 Book*
Printer: *R. R. Donnelley & Sons Company*

Library of Congress Cataloging-in-Publication Data

Elbow, Peter.
     Sharing and responding, Third edition/Peter Elbow, Pat Belanoff.
        p. cm.
     ISBN 0-07-303179-8 (pbk.: acid-free paper)
     1. English language — Rhetoric.   2. Report writing.   I. Title.   II. Belanoff, Pat.
PE1408.E385   2000
808'.04221—dc21   99-043523

http://www.mhhe.com

Peter Elbow

Peter Elbow is Professor of English and Director of the Writing Program at the University of Massachusetts at Amherst. Before writing *A Community of Writers,* he wrote two other books about writing: *Writing Without Teachers* and *Writing with Power: Techniques for Mastering the Writing Process.* He is author of a book of essays about learning and teaching, *Embracing Contraries,* in addition to *What Is English?,* which explores current issues in the profession of English, *Oppositions in Chaucer,* and numerous essays about writing and teaching. His most recent book is *Writing For—Not Against: Essays on Writing and the Teaching of Writing.*

He has taught at the Massachusetts Institute of Technology, Franconia College, Evergreen State College, and the State University of New York at Stony Brook—where for five years he directed the Writing Program. He served for four years on the Executive Council of the Modern Language Association and was a member of the Executive Committee of the Conference on College Composition and Communication. He has given talks and workshops at many colleges and universities.

He attended Williams College and Harvard University and has an M.A. from Exeter College, Oxford University, and a Ph.D. from Brandeis University.

Pat Belanoff

Pat Belanoff is Associate Professor of English at the State University of New York–Stony Brook. She has been both president of the SUNY Council on Writing and a member of the College Steering Committee of NCTE. Pat is a coauthor (with Betsy Rorschach and Mia Oberlink) of *The Right Handbook,* now in its second edition. She has also coedited (with Marcia Dickson) *Portfolios: Process and Product* and (with Peter Elbow and Sheryl Fontaine) *Nothing Begins With an N: New Investigations of Freewriting.* Pat has a doctorate in medieval literature from New York University and continues to teach and publish in this area, too.

When Peter Elbow published *Writing Without Teachers* in 1973, peer response groups were little known and the idea of students working by themselves to give one another feedback about their writing tended to be dismissed as "the blind leading the blind." Since that time, however, peer feedback or response has come to be accepted by most teachers and theorists as useful and important to the teaching of writing. Yet even now textbooks don't give much specific and detailed help to students for engaging in this far-from-straightforward activity. And students sometimes think of peer feedback as merely an idiosyncratic, experimental activity that their particular teacher happens to like.

Countless teachers have learned that it's no good saying blithely, "OK. Now get into groups and give feedback to each other." Trying it this way—without preparation and sustained help—has led many teachers to announce, "I tried peer response groups and they just don't work!"

We've written this *Sharing and Responding* booklet to remedy these problems. Students *can* give each other remarkably useful and productive feedback on their writing. But most of them need substantive help and instruction in learning to do so. And students usually do better when they see this help laid out carefully in a published book, not just in teacher handouts and oral instructions.

In this booklet, we have gathered together a full and detailed sequence of suggestions for students to use in sharing their writing with each other and giving and receiving useful responses. Originally this booklet was just a section of our textbook, *A Community of Writers,* but we soon realized that what we had written would be useful even to teachers who didn't want to use our textbook. We've learned that teachers with the widest range of diverse styles and approaches to the teaching of writing often want their students to learn to use peer response. (In addition to being a separate booklet, "Sharing and Responding" is also included as a part of the third edition of *A Community of Writers.*

We found that our first and second editions of *Sharing and Responding* tempted some teachers, who had been reluctant to do so or who had had unfortunate experiences with it, to try peer responding. For there is often something messy and potentially chaotic about using peer groups. One is always trying to shout one last suggestion while students are moving into pairs or groups, and chairs are scraping, and the hubbub of talk is taking over. *"Oh yes, and don't forget . . ."*—but they don't hear. And one is always running to the photocopy machine at the last minute to copy directions and suggestions. Of course nothing will ever make peer response groups tidy and quiet (we wouldn't want to), but we find this booklet helpful as a way to give our students more specific help: explanations, examples, guidelines, and principles for the complex feedback process.

When we use these techniques for peer responding, we sometimes ask students to work in pairs, sometimes in small groups. We sometimes change groups during the course term; often we stick with stable pairs or groups so that students can safely build up trust in each other. We sometimes try for both goals by keeping permanent pairs throughout the school term, but occasionally shifting the *pairings* of pairs into groups of four. Before sending students into pairs or groups for peer response, we tend to illustrate and practice each response technique in the whole class on one or two sample texts. We also like being able to ask students to read about a feedback process *for homework* before we practice it in class.

There are many more techniques in this booklet than a student or teacher could use all the time. Our principle in writing the booklet (and in our teaching) is this: Students need to *try out* a wide spectrum of ways to respond to a text in order to end up finally in the best position to *choose,* on any particular occasion, what kind of feedback to ask for or to give. Different kinds of response are suitable for different writers, different kinds of writing, and for different audience situations.

Peter Elbow
Pat Belanoff

Sharing and Responding

Sharing and Responding

Cover Letter

Dear Students and Teachers,

In this "Sharing and Responding" guide we present a variety of methods for sharing your writing and getting helpful responses. First we'll give a brief overview of the methods; then we'll explain them in more detail and illustrate their use on two sample essays.

Our goal is to help you become comfortable and skilled at asking for feedback and giving it. We think this may well be the most valuable part of the *Community of Writers* workshop course, the part you are most likely to use after the course is over.

Suggestions for Using "Sharing and Responding"

There are more techniques here than you can use on any one occasion. But we want you to try them all out in order to learn the wide range of options you have for feedback. Then you will be in a position to ask for the kind of feedback that is right for you, depending on your preferences or temperament, the kind of piece you're working on, and the stage it's at. Many people don't like getting feedback on their writing because they feel they are "on the chopping block." They don't realize how many options they could ask for, and so they end up helplessly putting themselves in the hands of readers. "Sharing and Responding" will help you take charge of the process of getting responses.

We also urge you to try out these techniques in order. They go from quicker to more time-consuming, from easier to harder, and from safer to riskier. This progression builds a feedback situation of support and trust. Don't assume, though, that the later kinds of responding are better: Some of the earliest ones remain the most useful despite being quick and easy.

Our Underlying Premises and Convictions

We find that most students are reluctant to judge or evaluate each other's writing and give advice about how to improve it. We think they are right. Evaluation and advice are not what writers need most. What writers need (and fortunately it's what all readers are best at) is an *audience*: a thoughtful, interested audience rather than evaluators or editors or advice-givers. In the long run, you will learn the most about writing from feeling the *presence of interested readers*—like feeling the weight of a fish at the end of the line. You can't trust evaluations or advice. Even experts on writing usually disagree with each other. And even when they agree about what is weak, they often disagree about how to fix it.

Therefore we urge you to follow a crucial principle for feedback: Don't let anyone give you evaluation or advice unless they also give you the perceptions and reactions it is based on, that is, unless they describe *what they see* and *how they are reacting*. For example, if a reader says, "The organization is confusing in your piece," make sure she goes back and describes the sequence of parts in your piece as she sees them, and/or the sequence of her reactions as she was reading: When did she first start feeling confused, and what kind of confusion was it? What was going on in her mind and feelings at different points?

Many students have never written except in school, never given their writing to anyone but a teacher, and always gotten some kind of evaluative response. But it's hard for writers to prosper unless they give their work to a variety of readers, not just teachers, and get a variety of responses: no response, nonevaluative responses, evaluative responses. The suggestions here will give you the variety of audience relationships you need to develop a more productive sense of audience.

You will improve your writing much faster if you let us and your teacher help you build a community in your classroom: a place where people hear clearly even what is mumbled, understand what is badly written, and look for the validity even in what they disagree with. Eventually you will learn to write to the enemy—to write surrounded by sharks. But you will learn that necessary skill better if, for a while, you practice writing to allies and listening to friends.

Two Paradoxes of Responding

First paradox: the reader is always right; yet the writer is always right. That is, readers get to decide what's true about their reactions—about what they see or think or feel. It's senseless to quarrel with readers about their experience of what's happening to them (though you can ask them to explain their experience more fully).

Nevertheless, you as the writer get to decide what to do about any of this feedback from readers, what changes to make, if any. You don't have to follow their advice. Just listen openly and swallow it all. You can do that better if you realize that you get to take your time and make up your own mind.

Second paradox: the writer must be in charge; yet the writer must sit quietly and do nothing. As writer, you must be in control. It's your writing. Don't be passive or helpless. You get to decide what kind of feedback, if any, you need. Are you trying to improve this particular piece? Or perhaps you don't care so much about working on this piece any more but just want feedback on it to learn about your writing in general. Or perhaps you don't want to work on anything but just enjoy sharing this piece and hearing what others have to say. Don't let readers make these decisions for you. Ask for what you want and don't be afraid to stop them if they give you the wrong thing. For example, sometimes it's important to insist, "I'm still very tender about this piece. I just want to hear what it sounds like for now and not get any feedback."

Nevertheless you mostly have to sit back and just listen. If you are talking a lot, you are probably blocking good feedback. For example, don't argue if they misunderstand what you wrote. Their misunderstanding is valuable, and you need to understand it in order to see how your words function. If they want to give you feedback you didn't ask for—or not give you what you ask for—they may have good reasons. If you aren't getting honest, serious, or caring feedback, don't blame your readers. You may not have convinced them that you really want it.

How We Wrote "Sharing and Responding"

In our first drafts of the *Community of Writers* book, we put all our sharing and responding suggestions in the workshops themselves. But then we ran into a dilemma. We realized that we wanted to give students and teachers lots of choice of which workshops to use and what order to use them in. Yet we didn't want to give that much choice about which feedback techniques to use and which order to use them in. For it's crucial to us that you go through a progression that gives the best learning and builds the most trust. Because of this dilemma, we hit on the plan of having a separate "Sharing and Responding" guide (though we have also kept a few suggestions in each workshop).

Also, this part in the first edition of our textbook was too complicated: too many kinds of response were arranged in groupings which were too complex. We realize now that as we worked out this book for the first time, we built too much of our background thinking into the structure itself. Writers often speak of the principle of "scaffolding": structures put up in order to help construct the building in the first place—but which can be taken down after the building is done. We had too much scaffolding in the first edition. You'll find the same thing sometimes happens to you. You'll write something and it comes out complicated; but once you've got it written, you finally understand it better and you can then revise to make it simpler.

And, now for this third edition, we have changed the sample essays. Some of our students and reviewers told us it would be helpful to have essays on topics more relevant to today's world and the kinds of problems they might meet up with in their own lives. We think the two essays we selected confront such problems. We hope you agree. But whether you do or don't, we'd like to have responses from you since, like you, we can profit from readers' responses. Please feel free to comment on any part of this textbook. (You can write to us at the publisher's address.)

Peter Elbow
Pat Belanoff

Summary of Kinds of Responses

Here is an overview of 11 different and valuable ways of responding to writing and a few thoughts about when each kind is valuable. We will explain them more fully later and illustrate their use on sample essays. After you have tried them out, you can glance back over this list when you want to decide which kind of feedback to request.

1. Sharing: No Response

Read your piece aloud to listeners and ask: "Would you please just listen and enjoy?" You can also give them your text to read silently, though you don't usually learn as much this way. Simple sharing is also a way to listen better to your own responses to your own piece, without having to think about how others respond. You learn an enormous amount from hearing yourself read your own words or from reading them over when you know that someone else is also reading them.

No response is valuable in many situations—when you don't have much time, at very early stages when you want to try something out or feel very tentative, or when you are completely finished and don't plan to make any changes at all—as a form of simple communication or celebration. Sharing gives you an unpressured setting for getting comfortable reading your words out loud and listening to the writing of others.

2. Pointing and Center of Gravity

Pointing: "Which words or phrases or passages somehow strike you? stick in mind? get through?" Center of gravity: "Which sections somehow seem important or resonant or generative?" You are not asking necessarily for the main points but for sections or passages that seem to resonate or linger in mind. Sometimes a seemingly minor detail or example—even an aside or a digression—can be a center of gravity.

These quick, easy, interesting forms of response are good for timid or inexperienced responders, or for early drafts. They help you establish a sense of contact with readers. Center of gravity response is particularly interesting for showing you rich and interesting parts of your piece that you might have neglected, but which might be worth exploring and developing. Center of gravity can help you see your piece in a different light and suggest ways to make major revisions.

3. Summary and Sayback

Summary: "Please summarize what you have heard. Tell me what you hear as the main thing and the almost-main things." (Variations: "Give me a phrase as title and a one-word title—first using my words and then using your words.") Sayback: "Please say back to me in your own words what you hear me getting at in my piece, but say it in a somewhat questioning or tentative way—as an invitation for me to reply with my own restatement of what you've said."

These are both useful at any stage in the writing process to see whether readers "got" the points you are trying to "give." But sayback is particularly useful at early stages when you are still groping and haven't yet been able to find what you really want to say. You can read a collection of exploratory passages for sayback response. When readers say back to you what they hear—and invite you to reply—it often leads you to find exactly the words or thoughts or emphasis you were looking for.

4. What Is Almost Said? What Do You Want to Hear More About?

Just ask readers those very questions.

This kind of response is particularly useful when you need to *develop* or enrich your piece—when you sense there is more here but you haven't been able to get your finger on it yet. This kind of question gives you concrete substantive help because it leads your readers to give you some of *their ideas* to add to yours. Remember this too: What you imply but don't say in your writing is often very loud to readers but unheard by you and has an enormous effect on how they respond.

Extreme variation: "Make a guess about what was on my mind that I didn't write about."

5. Reply

Simply ask, "What are *your* thoughts about my topic? Now that you've heard what I've had to say, what do *you* have to say?"

This kind of response is useful at any point, but it is particularly useful at early stages when you haven't worked out your thinking. Indeed, you can ask for this kind of response even before you've written a draft; perhaps you jotted down some notes. You can say, "I'm thinking about saying *X*, *Y*, and *Z*. How would you reply? What are your thoughts about this topic?" This is actually the most natural and common response to any human discourse. You are inviting a small discussion of the topic.

6. Voice

(a) "How much voice do you hear in my writing? Is my language alive and human? Or is it dead, bureaucratic, unsayable?" (b) "What kind of voice(s) do you hear in my writing? Timid? Confident? Sarcastic? Pleading?" Or "What kind of person does my writing sound like? What side(s) of me come through in my writing?" Most of all, "Do you trust the voice or person you hear in my writing?"

This kind of feedback can be useful at any stage. When people describe the voice they hear in writing, they often get right to the heart of subtle but important matters of language and approach. They don't have to be able to talk in technical terms ("You seem to use lots of passive verbs and nominalized phrases"); they can say, "You sound kind of bureaucratic and pompous and I wonder if you actually believe what you are saying."

7. Movies of the Reader's Mind

Ask readers to tell you honestly and in detail what is going on in their minds as they read your words. There are three powerful ways to help readers give you this kind of response: (a) Interrupt their reading a few times and find out what's happening at that moment. (b) Get them to tell you their reactions in the form of a *story* that takes place in time. (c) If they make "it-statements" ("It was confusing"), make them translate these into "I-statements" ("I felt confused starting here about . . .").

Movies of the reader's mind make the most sense when you have a fairly developed draft and you want to know how it works on readers, rather than when you're still trying to develop your ideas. Movies are the richest and most valuable form of response, but they require that you feel some confidence in yourself and support from your reader, because when readers tell you honestly what is happening while they are reading your piece, they may tell you they don't like it or even get mad at it.

8. Metaphorical Descriptions

Ask readers to describe your writing in terms of clothing (e.g., jeans, tuxedo, lycra running suit), weather (e.g., foggy, stormy, sunny, humid), animals, colors, shapes.

This kind of response is helpful at any point. It gives you a new view, a new lens; it's particularly helpful when you feel stale on a piece, perhaps because you have worked so long on it. Sometimes young or inexperienced readers are good at giving you this kind of response when they are unskilled at other kinds.

9. Believing and Doubting

Believing: "Try to believe everything I have written, even if you disagree or find it crazy. At least *pretend* to believe it. Be my friend and ally and give me more evidence, arguments, and ideas to help me make my case better." Doubting: "Try to doubt everything I have written, even if you love it. Take on the role of enemy and find all the arguments that can be made against me. Pretend to be someone who hates my writing. What would he or she notice?"

These forms of feedback obviously lend themselves to persuasive essays or arguments, though the believing game can help you flesh out and enrich the world of a story or poem. Believing is good when you are struggling and want help. It's a way to get readers to give you new ideas and arguments and to improve your piece in all sorts of ways. Doubting is good after you've gotten a piece as strong as you can get it and you want to send it out or hand it in—but first find out how hostile readers will fight you.

10. Skeleton Feedback and Descriptive Outline

Skeleton feedback: "Please lay out the reasoning you see in my paper: my main point, my subpoints, my supporting evidence, and my assumptions about my topic and about my audience." Descriptive outline: "Please write *says* and *does* sentences for my whole paper and then for each paragraph or section." A *says* sentence summarizes the meaning or message, and a *does* sentence describes the function.

These are the most useful for essays. They are feasible only if the reader has the text in hand and can take a good deal of time and care—and perhaps write out responses. Because they give you the most distance and perspective on what you have written, they are uniquely useful for giving feedback to yourself. Both kinds of feedback help you on late drafts when you want to test out your reasoning and organization. But skeleton feedback is also useful on early drafts when you are still trying to figure out what to say or emphasize and how to organize your thoughts.

11. Criterion-Based Feedback

Ask readers to give you their thoughts about specific criteria that you are wondering about or struggling with: "Does this sound too technical?" "Is this section too long?" "Do my jokes work for you?" "Do you feel I've addressed the objections of people who disagree?" And of course, "Please find mistakes in spelling and grammar and typing." You can also ask readers to address what they think are the important criteria for your piece. You can ask too about traditional criteria for essays: focus on the assignment or task, content (ideas, reasoning, support, originality), organization, clarity of language, and voice.

You ask for criterion-based feedback when you have questions about specific aspects of your piece. You can also ask for it when you need a quick overview of strengths and weaknesses. This kind of feedback depends on skilled and experienced readers. (But even with them you should still take it with a grain of salt, for if someone says your piece is boring, other readers might well disagree. Movies of the reader's mind are more trustworthy because they give you a better picture of the personal reactions *behind* these judgments.)

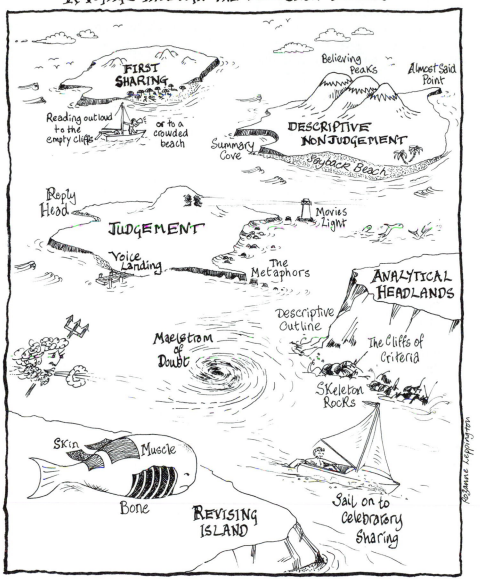

A VOYAGE THROUGH THE FEEDBACK ISLANDS

Procedures for Giving and Receiving Responses

We've briefly summarized your choices among *kinds of response*. Now we want to emphasize that you also have important choices among *procedures for getting responses*. It's important to test these out, too—to see which ones are the most helpful for you in different situations.

Early or Late Drafts?

Responses are helpful on both early and late drafts; indeed, it's a big help to discuss your thinking even before you have written at all. (For very early drafts, these response modes are particularly helpful: pointing, center of gravity, summary, sayback, almost said, and reply.) At the other extreme, it can be helpful and interesting to get feedback even on *final drafts* that you don't plan to revise any more: You will learn about your writing and about how readers read. When poets and fiction writers give readings, the goal is pleasure and celebration, not feedback. (Keep your eye out for notices of readings by poets and writers in local schools, libraries, and bookstores. They can be fun to attend.)

Pairs or Groups?

On the one hand, the more readers the better. Readers are different, and reading is a subjective act so you don't know much if you only know how one reader reacts. On the other hand, more readers take more time and you can learn a lot from one reader if she is a good one—if she can really tell you in detail about what she sees and what goes on in her head as she reads your words. Also, it's easier to build an honest relationship of trust and support between just two people. (If you know you are working on something important and will want to get feedback at various stages, you can use your trusted readers one or two at a time.)

You can have it both ways too—getting the multiple perspectives of groups and the trust and support of pairs—by first getting brief feedback from a group and then dividing into pairs for fuller responses (or vice versa).

New Faces or the Same Old Faces?

If you change readers, you get variety and new perspectives. But good sharing and responding depend on a climate of safety and trust. Certain things can't occur until reader and writer have built up trust, and that takes longer than you might think. Most writers find one or two trusted readers or editors, and rely on them over and over.

Share Out Loud or Give Readers Copies on Paper?

The process of reading out loud brings important learning: You can feel strengths and weaknesses physically—in your mouth as you pronounce your words and in your ear as you hear them. And you can tell about the effects of your words by watching your listeners. Reading out loud is more alive. But if your piece is very long or time is short, you will need to give paper copies. Paper texts give readers more time to read closely and reflect on your writing, especially if the material is technical. Remember, however, that if listeners can't follow your piece as you read it out loud, it is probably not clear enough.

Perhaps the most efficient way to get the most feedback in the shortest time is to circulate paper copies around a group; at every moment, everyone is reading someone's paper and writing feedback. (You have the choice of whether to let readers see how previous readers responded.) But efficiency is not everything; this method is not very sociable. You can also combine the two modalities by reading your paper out loud but giving listeners a copy to follow. (Computers and photocopy machines make it easier to create multiple copies.)

Writers have always used the mail to share writing with readers and get responses, but electronic mail and fax machines have encouraged many more people to "meet" across hundreds and thousands of miles. Some people use these media not just for transmitting pieces of writing and responses but even for "real time" conversation about the writing.

About Reading Out Loud

You need to read your piece twice. Otherwise listeners can't hear it well enough to give helpful responses. But if you don't want to read it twice in a row (which can feel embarrassing), there is a good solution. Have each person read once for no response; then have each person read again for response. Listeners need a bit of silence after each reading to collect their thoughts and jot down a few notes; this way no one will be too influenced later by hearing the responses of others.

Also, it can be interesting and useful to have the second reading given by someone other than the writer. This way listeners get to hear two different "versions" of the words. When someone reads a piece of writing out loud, that in itself constitutes feedback: it reveals a great deal about what the reader sees as the meaning, emphasis, implications, and voice or tone of the piece. Some critics and writers say that a set of words is not "realized" or "complete" until read out loud—that words on the page are like a play script or musical notes on a page, mere ingredients for the creation of the real thing, which is a performance.

Some writers get others to give both readings, but we think that's sad because you learn so much from reading your own words. If you feel very shy or even afraid to read your writing, that means it's even more important to do so.

Responding Out Loud or on Paper?

Both modes are valuable. Spoken responses are easier to give, more casual and social. And it's interesting for responders to hear the responses of the others. Written responses can be more careful and considered, and the writer gets to take them home and ponder them while revising.

There's an easy way to combine written and spoken responding. First, all group members give copies of their paper to everyone else. Then members go home and read all the papers and take a few notes about their responses to each one. But each member has responsibility for giving a careful written response to only one paper. When the group meets for sharing responses, the person who wrote out feedback starts by reading what he wrote (and hands his written feedback to the writer), but then the others chime in and add responses on the basis of their reading and notes. This method is particularly useful if there isn't much time for group work or if the pieces of writing are somewhat long.

How Much Response to Get?

At one extreme, you'll benefit from no response at all—that is, from private writing where you get to ignore readers for a while, and from mere sharing where you get to connect with readers and feel their presence but not have to listen to their responses.

At the other extreme, it's crucial sometimes to take the time for extended and careful response—perhaps in writing—from at least one or two readers. We urge you to create some occasions where you ask a reader or two to take your paper home and write out at least two or three pages that provide (a) a description of what they see (skeleton or descriptive outline, description of voice, and so forth); (b) a description of how they reacted (movies of their minds—what the words *do* to them); (c) what they see as strengths and weaknesses of your paper and suggestions for improving it. If your teacher asks for this extensive approach to feedback, she will probably ask you to write out your reactions to those responses, in particular whether you think their evaluation and advice make sense or not and why.

A middle course is to get two to four minutes of response from each reader. This won't give you the complete story of the readers' perceptions or reactions, but it will give you the most powerful thing of all: the leverage you need to imagine what your piece of writing looks like through someone else's eyes. Sometimes just one tiny remark is all you need to help you suddenly stop seeing your words *only* from your own point of view and start experiencing how differently they sound to someone else.

Ways to Help Response Pairs or Groups Work Better

When it comes to people working together on difficult activities (and nothing is more "difficult" than showing your own writing), there are no magic right methods. But there are some helpful rules of thumb.

First, remember that even though you may feel naked or vulnerable in sharing your writing, especially if it is an early draft, readers will be just as naked and vulnerable if they give you good feedback. To give accurate movies of the mind is a generous gift: honest readers are willing to be guinea pigs and let you see inside their heads. And this kind of honesty goes against many habits and customs of student life. Classmates won't give you this gift unless you treat them with great respect *and* are very assertive about insisting that you really want good feedback. (As teachers, we used to shake our fingers at students who weren't giving much feedback and try to cajole them into being "more responsible responders." But that never seemed to help. We discovered we could get better results by turning back to the *writer* and saying: "Are *you* willing to put up with not getting feedback? *We* can't make them do it. Only *you* can.")

Try to avoid arguments between responders or between writer and responder. Arguments waste time, and they make responders less willing to be honest. But most of all, you usually benefit from having different and unreconciled points of view about your text. Don't look for a "right answer" but for how your writing looks through different sets of eyes. And when readers disagree, that brings home the central principle here: *You* get to make up your own mind about how to interpret the feedback, how seriously to take it, and what changes to make, if any.

When working in groups, always make sure someone agrees to watch the time so that people at the end don't get cheated.

Spend some time talking about how the feedback process is working. Try taking a few moments now and then to write out informal answers to these questions.

- What works best in your group?
- What is not working well?
- Do you wish members were more critical of your work? less critical?
- Which has been the most helpful to you, oral or written responses?
- Does your group work best with detailed instructions? with little guidance?
- Is there someone who always seems to take charge? or who doesn't participate much? How do you feel about this?

You can share these responses yourselves and identify problems and discuss ways to make things work better. You can make these comments anonymous if you wish by giving them to another group to read to you. Your teacher may ask for these responses and use them as a basis for full-class discussion.

Final Note

Does this seem too complicated? All these kinds of responses and ways of giving them? There is, in fact, a lot to learn if you want to get useful responses and give them. But *after* you and your friends have tried out all these techniques and built up a relationship of trust, you can make the whole feedback process become simple. You don't have to decide on any particular kind of feedback to ask for; you can just say, "Tell me about your responses" or "Just write me a letter." You can trust them to give you what is most valuable. But if you leave it wide open this way *before* readers have practiced all these responding techniques, you often get nothing—or even get something hurtful or harmful. It won't take you too long to try out the 11 kinds of feedback, especially since you can sometimes use more than one in one session.

Full Explanations of Kinds of Responses—With Samples*

1. Sharing: No Response or Responses from the Self

If you've never done freewriting before—writing without stopping and not showing your words to anyone at all—it can feel peculiar. But most people quickly find it comfortable and helpful. Similarly, if you've never done sharing before—reading your words to someone without getting any response at all—that too can feel peculiar. When you read your words aloud (or give people a copy of your writing), you probably have an urge to ask them how they *liked* it—whether they thought it was any good. Because all school writing is evaluated, we sometimes assume that the *point* of writing is to be evaluated. But when we speak to someone, do we immediately ask them how good our words were? No. We want a reply, not an evaluation. We speak because we are trying to communicate and connect.

With sharing we're emphasizing writing as communicating and connecting, rather than performing for a judgment. You'll find that it's a relief to give your writing to others (aloud or on paper) just to communicate, just for the fun of it—so they can hear what you have to say and learn from you. It's a relief to say (on some occasions, anyway), "The hell with whether they like it or agree with it. I just want them to *hear* it." If you practice sharing in the right spirit, you will soon find it as natural and helpful as freewriting.

And what is the right spirit? In sharing, the goal is for writers to *give* and for listeners to *receive*. Writing is gift giving. When you give someone a gift, you don't want her to criticize; you want her to use it and enjoy it. If you happen to give someone a gift he doesn't like, do you want him to complain? No, you want him to thank you all the same.

We stress reading your words aloud here, especially at first, because you learn so much by using your mouth and ears. And there is a special psychological benefit from learning to say your words aloud: You get over the fear of making a noise with your written words. But it is also useful to share silently, by giving readers a copy of what you've written. Many teachers periodically create a class magazine. Sometimes they set this up officially with a lab fee to cover costs; sometimes they just ask everyone to bring in multiple copies of a piece. If you single-space your piece, you can often fit it on one sheet,

---

*For sample peer responses, we are indebted to Alexander Jackson, Arun Jacob Rao, Christine Schnaitter, and others.

back-to-back. Also, you'll find it a pleasure to make a little magazine at the end of the course of your favorite three or four pieces of your own writing (with a nice cover), and give copies to a handful of friends and family.

We suggested earlier that as you try out different kinds of feedback, you might try out more than one kind in one session. But don't combine sharing with feedback (not at first, anyway). The whole point of sharing is to get *no* response. Even if it feels odd at first, try to notice the benefits of it.

Guidelines for the Writer Who Is Sharing Aloud

- Take a moment to look at your listeners, relax, and take a deep breath. Say a few introductory words if that helps.
- Read slowly, clearly. *Own* your writing; read it with authority even if you are not satisfied with it. Concentrate on the meaning of what you're reading. Don't worry about whether listeners like it.
- Take a pause between paragraphs. Let people interrupt to ask you to repeat or go slower, but don't let them give you any feedback. After you're finished, just go on to the next person.

Guidelines for Listeners

- Your job is to receive without comment. Give no feedback of any kind.
- If the writer is racing or mumbling so you can't understand, interrupt him appreciatively but firmly, and ask him to read more slowly and clearly.
- When the writer has finished reading, thank her and go on to the next person. If there is time after everyone has read, you might want to hear the pieces again—especially the more complex ones. Or you might agree to discuss the *topics,* but don't let the discussion turn into feedback on each other's writing.

Exploring the Writing Process

I felt good about reading my piece of writing to the response group yesterday. It was good for me to be in control, by being able to specify what kind of response I wanted to receive. One thing that frightens me as a writer reading my stuff, is that once it's out there, I'm terribly vulnerable. It is often like sharing a secret part of myself. Or like giving birth. As long as the idea stays within me, it is protected, but once it is "born," it is vulnerable. I think of getting my Shakespeare paper back from M. with the *B+* and the marks all over it. I had a very hard time starting the next paper. I didn't trust my ability. I felt the unseen censor's heavy presence. I know that his intentions were to help me to improve my writing, but my problem was to get past the roadblock of my damaged ego [. . .]. I can't change how the world deals with my writing, so maybe the key is in working on my own attitude toward the criticism I get.

Jo Ferrell

2. Pointing and Center of Gravity

These two kinds of feedback fit well with two readings of your piece. After the first reading, listeners can point to the words and phrases that struck them or seemed most memorable. This is a way of letting a writer know which bits of his writing got through or made the strongest impression.

Then after each person's second reading, listeners can tell where they sense any *centers of gravity:* spots they sense as generative centers or sources of energy in the text. They might not be main points. Sometimes an image, phrase, detail, or digression seems a point of special life or weight in the piece.

When you read, don't rush, even though you might feel nervous. Allow a bit of silence after each reading. Give listeners time to collect their impressions.

Why Would Anyone Want Wholly Descriptive Feedback without Criticism or Advice?

This and the next two kinds of response ("Summary and Sayback" and "What Is Almost Said?") ask for description without evaluation or suggestions. If this feels odd, consider the following reasons:

- We benefit most from feedback on *early* drafts, but it doesn't make sense to evaluate an early draft. When we put off feedback until after we've slaved over something, it's hard to revise because we've invested too much sweat and blood. Nonjudgmental feedback gives us early feedback and new ideas and simply ignores the fact that, of course, there are obvious problems in our early draft. It makes readers into allies rather than adversaries while they help us see our still evolving text better and give us new insights.

- Perhaps we're trying out a new kind of writing or an approach that we're weak at: We're trying to break out of the rut of what we can already do well. Or we're working on something so difficult but important that we don't want criticism yet. We just need some *perspective* on our piece. We need a reader to trust us, to trust that we can see faults ourselves and work through them. And frankly we also need some encouragement and support in seeing what's right or strong in the piece.

- We may want feedback from someone who is a good reader but who can only criticize. It's her only gear. We need her perceptions but not her knife. Asking for descriptive responses is a way to nudge her out of her judgmental rut.

- We often need to give feedback to a weak or inexperienced writer or to a writer in a rut. Often we sense that criticism and "helpful advice" are not what he needs. Sure, his writing has serious problems, but what he needs is encouragement and confidence. We often sense that the very thing that's been undermining his writing is too much criticism: He's been clenching too hard; he's been criticizing and rewriting every phrase as he writes it until all the energy and clarity are gone from his writing. He'll write better when he trusts himself better. Nonjudgmental feedback will help.

SAMPLES OF FEEDBACK: POINTING AND CENTER OF GRAVITY

The sample essays will be found on pages 49–53.

Pointing for "What's Wrong with Black English?":
One Reader:

- Big saggy pants and knit caps.
- America is cool.
- Blacks of America and their culture have the power of attracting people.
- Banning Black English and forcing them to learn Standard English only hurts the children's identity because it means to the children that their language and culture are rejected in the public place.
- "Children have the right to their own language." This is a quote used in the paper, but it is strong and direct and stands out.
- Feelings of public separateness do not come from the language only.
- The advocates of nonbilingual education may believe that the only culture in this country should be the one of the dominant white middle class.

Another Reader:

- Black children should be taught both in Black English (Ebonics) and the Standard English.
- Forcing them to learn Standard English only hurts the children's identity.
- Their language and culture are rejected.
- Children have the right to their own language.
- Language is a culture.
- If you lose your language, you lose the way of expressing yourself.
- Standard English . . . white middle class rules and codes are necessary tools for success.
- Like it or not, they [the white middle class] mark the place where "power" currently exists.
- The reason people love America is its diversity.
- Melting pot of many ethnic groups.
- Coming from the racially homogeneous country like Japan, I see the standardization of America as a great loss to today's diversified world.

Pointing for "The Power of Sprinkles":
One Reader:

- I don't want to do this.
- Our GPA will suffer.
- E-mail isn't the same.
- If you can write for that then why can't you write for this?

Another Reader:

- I don't want to do this I don't want to do this I don't want to do this!
- We have to do this.
- I hate writing!
- You argue all the time.

- Stupid messages aren't just stupid—they're fun!
- And what about the diary?
- It doesn't count.
- Well, if you can write for that, why can't you write for this?
- Because this is assigned!
- Minimum length is good. It tells us how much detail we're supposed to go into and how much we should say about something.
- Adding more would make it worse. It's hard putting in bull_ _ _ _.
- We never do things my way.
- We don't always have to do things the way we're supposed to. Sometimes it works much better if we do our own thing, and just make it look like what it's supposed to be.
- As soon as it's over, we can get a Smurf sundae.
- With sprinkles?
- Of course.
- It's a deal. Let's get started.

<u>Centers of Gravity</u> for "What's Wrong with Black English?":
One Reader:

- The image of Japanese kids with baggy sagging pants and girls braiding their hair with beads and huge crowds dancing to rap music.
- Vicious circle of uneducated, poor, single mothers and lives depending on the welfare.
- Destroying a language is destroying people.
- In the 19th century, many people came to the New World because they saw this country as a melting pot of many ethnic groups, and they thought there would be room for them to live their lives.

Another Reader:

- When the bilingually educated blacks are the majority of the black population of America, it will again change white people's ways of thinking and the history of the country.
- Advocates of nonbilingual education may believe that the only culture in this country should be the one of the dominant white middle class.
- The reason people love America is its diversity.

<u>Centers of Gravity</u> for "The Power of Sprinkles":
One Reader:

- Examples the writer gives to demonstrate the necessity for communication in life.
- Reasons why students get marked down on papers.
- Reasons why writing for an assignment is not fun.

Another Reader:

- The fact that essays don't have to be long and boring. You can use your imagination to have fun while writing essays.
- Sprinkles.

3. Summary and Sayback

These two kinds of response are similar. Try them both and see which one feels more useful to you (or perhaps work out some combination of the two). If your piece is not too long or complex, you can get summary feedback after the first reading and sayback after the second. (If your piece is long or complex, you need two readings even for summary feedback.)

Summary is a way to find out how readers understand your words—whether your message got through. Many needless misunderstandings come about because readers are arguing about the strengths or weaknesses of someone's ideas without realizing they have different interpretations of what the piece is saying. The procedure is simple: Ask readers for a one-sentence summary, a one-phrase summary, and a one-word summary. (You can even ask for two versions of these summaries: one version that uses words from your writing and one where listeners must use their own language.) Another way to ask: "Give me a couple of titles for this piece."

Sayback (or active listening) is a simple but subtle variation. The author reads and the listener "says back" what she hears the writer "getting at." But she says it back in a slightly open, questioning fashion in order to invite the writer to restate what she means. In effect the listener is saying, "Do you mean. . . ?" so that the writer can say, "No, not quite. What I mean is . . ." Or "Yes, but let me put it this way . . ." Or even—and this is pay dirt—"Yes, I *was* saying that, but *now* I want to say . . ." Sayback helped her move past her original thinking.

In short, sayback is an invitation to the writer to find new words and thoughts—to move in her thinking. Sayback helps the writing continue to cook, bubble, percolate. It helps the writer think about what she hasn't yet said or even thought of.

Thus, though sayback is useful any time, it is particularly useful at an early stage in your writing when you have only written in an exploratory way and things haven't jelled yet.

Here's an important variation: *Sayback to help you figure out what you are doing.* Get your listener to tell what he senses as your *goals* (the effects you want your writing to have) and your *strategies* (how you want to achieve those effects with language). Use his guesses as a springboard to help you talk out your goals and strategies for this piece. The best thing for revising is to get clearer in your mind what you're trying to accomplish and what language strategies you want to use. Take plenty of time to talk and take notes.*

To the Listener Giving Sayback

- Don't worry about whether you like or don't like something: That's irrelevant here. Listen and get engaged with what you hear.

---

*We are grateful to have learned about the use of sayback responding from Sondra Perl and Elaine Avidon of the New York City Writing Project.

- After listening, try to sum up in a sentence or two what you feel the writer is getting at. For sayback, say your response in a mildly questioning tone that invites the writer to respond. Think of yourself as inviting the writer to restate and thereby to get closer to what she really wants to say.

To the Writer Asking for Sayback

- Listen openly to the listener's sayback. If the listener seems to misunderstand what you have written, don't fight it. Use this misunderstanding as a spur to find new words for what you are really trying to say. The process of listening to a misunderstanding and then saying what you really mean often helps you find new key words and phrases that get right to the heart of the matter and prevent future misunderstanding.
- Don't feel stuck with what you've already written; don't defend it. Keep your mind open and receptive: think of this as help in shifting, adjusting, and refining your thinking.

SAMPLES OF FEEDBACK: SUMMARY AND SAYBACK

Summary for "What's Wrong with Black English?":
One Reader:

- Black English is very important and it should also be taught to black children together with standard English.

Another Reader:

- You admonish whites and society for saying that Black English is bad. It is useful and is part of the cultural identity of a portion of the people; thus it should be taught in schools. This is a part of the cultural diversity that makes America great.

Summary for "The Power of Sprinkles":
One Reader:

- The statement behind this essay is that sometimes it is hard to write, especially when you are told to. You may feel like you want to put it off or not bother. But it serves a purpose. A good way to write is to say what you know and feel, and then mold that into what is required. You may have to bribe yourself, but if that is what it takes to get you started, then do it.

Exploring the Writing Process

Group work is really interesting now. I never liked sharing before I took this class but now I even look forward to it. English was always not one of my better subjects, especially writing anything other than letters to my friends or opinion papers. I never wanted to share my writing because I felt stupid and like I wasn't a good writer. It's really easy to share my work now and I met great people in the class. Sharing and working together is a way to get to know people better and gives you a group of people that you can feel comfortable with and even become close friends with.

A Student

Another Reader:

- The writer talks the problem out in detail with herself, comes to a solution, and then moves on.

<u>Sayback</u> for "What's Wrong with Black English?":
One Reader:

- I hear you saying that Black English is very popular because some people in Japan like it? You are saying that it is going to be easy for black children to learn both kinds of English?

Another Reader:

- I understood the writer to be arguing in support of Ebonics in the classroom. The writer assumes Ebonics to be a language of Black Americans, and she asserts that although Ebonics is considered a lower class language, children should be taught it in schools so the children may gain confidence of their culture. The writer was stating that when the language of Blacks is rejected by society, it is a rejection of their culture in the American society. In the middle of the paper, the writer essentially argues that Blacks cannot communicate or express themselves through the English language, so they should be taught in Ebonics in order to gain cultural confidence. She concludes that bilingual education should be implemented in schools so Black culture can remain alive and strong and continue to add diversity to America.

<u>Sayback</u> for "The Power of Sprinkles":
One Reader:

- Writing can be a struggle. I hear you giving a picture of the opposing forces in all of us that promote procrastination, especially when we don't exactly want to do the work. Sometimes it is necessary to reason with ourselves to do something. A bribe may be necessary, but it is a small price to pay for the reward we get from a job well done. I wonder if you are implying that it may not work this way for everyone.

Another Reader:

- You are having an ongoing conversation with yourself, an internal dialogue complaining to yourself about why you hate to write. Your inner voice reminds you of the positive aspects of writing, how you write on an everyday basis, how writing skills are essential for communication in life. You agree with your inner voice but say that such daily writing is fun because you are free to say what you want; you wonder why teachers ask for extended "bull_ _ _ _." You talk about not being able to express your true opinions for fear of getting your grade docked by a disagreeing teacher. Toward the end, the two voices agree that you can be unique and dare to add creativity; sometimes when you do that, the finished product is much better because you invested yourself; you can add humor and silliness and the quality only improves.

4. What Is Almost Said? What Do You Want to Hear More About?

This response technique moves slightly away from what's in the text. No text can ever tell readers everything they need for understanding it; all texts assume that readers already know some of what the writer knows. Literary theorists speak of what's not there as "gaps." When readers respond to a piece of writing by telling you what's almost said or implied, they are telling you how they are filling in your gaps: what they feel hovering around the edges, what they feel you have assumed.

A surprisingly helpful and playful variation is to ask readers to guess what was on your mind that you *didn't* write about. This kind of feedback often gets at an undercurrent or mood or atmosphere that is only faintly present in your writing but which has an important subliminal effect on your readers.

SAMPLES OF FEEDBACK: WHAT IS ALMOST SAID? WHAT DO YOU WANT TO HEAR MORE ABOUT?

What Is Almost Said? for "What's Wrong with Black English?":
One Reader:

- Opponents of bilingual education are cultural suppressors who are striving to keep underclass blacks underclass.
- Teaching Black English in schools is the only way to help Blacks feel important in society.
- Standard English is white.
- Language keeps culture alive.

Another Reader:

- Communication and unity in the U.S. won't be harmed if Black English is taught.
- Japan and other countries don't have much diversity.
- You like to hear Black English.

What Is Almost Said? for "The Power of Sprinkles":
One Reader:

- Teachers like to make writing tedious, uncreative, boring.
- Restriction of creativity is oppression.
- Bribery works—even on yourself.
- A lot of students do an awful lot of writing other than what is assigned in school.
- To do anything well, you have to break the rules.
- To do anything well, you have to bribe and compromise.
- To do anything well, you have to get the different parts of yourself to work together cooperatively.

Another Reader:

- Writing essays can be like doing other common everyday things we do without thinking.
- Everyone consists of at least two people—a "we." You never need to be lonely.
- The voice that says you need to write is the real you.
- The voice that doesn't want to write is the real you.
- e.e.cummings has made a great literary impact and his poetry is limited by nothing.
- In life you don't just have to learn to get along with other people, you have to learn to get along with yourself.

What Do You Want to Hear More About for "What's Wrong with Black English?":
One Reader:

- How many schools are presently doing that? teaching bilingually?
- What is the dropout rate for Black students compared to white students?

- I assume Black English is a slang or loose form of regular English. You imply it's a whole language. Is this true? I'd like to hear more about this.
- I'd like to know the story of some particular students. What was it like when they couldn't use their own language? What was it like when they were invited to use their own language?

Another Reader:

- I'm interested in what you say in the 2nd paragraph: "When the bilingually educated Blacks consist of the majority of the Black population of America, it will again change the white people's ways of thinking and the history of this country." I want to hear how you think it will change people's thinking. How will the emergence of a middle class Black population influence others?
- What do you mean in the fifth paragraph when you say, ". . . an understanding of white middle class rules and codes are necessary tools for social success"? What rules and codes are you referring to specifically?

<u>**What Do You Want to Hear More About**</u> for "The Power of Sprinkles":
One Reader:

- What sort of essays do you write with "silly stuff"? How about using pictures for writing essays?
- What are some tricks for getting teachers to accept creative and silly and fun writing?
- It sounds like you basically enjoy writing—if the conditions are OK. Is that true? How did you manage that?

Another Reader:

- Do you often write dialogues in your head?
- Do you really have these dialogues silently in your head—or was this just a way to write something? Do you ever talk out loud to yourself?
- Which voice is most you? Or are they both equal?
- Can you use this technique about other difficulties, like whether to go out with someone?
- Which voice wins the most battles?

5. Reply

When you ask readers to reply to what you have written, you are asking for the most human and natural kind of response. And you are also asking readers to treat your writing in the most serious way: to engage with it at the level of substance. In effect, you are saying, "Please take my writing and my thinking seriously enough to reply to what I have said instead of ignoring or sidestepping my ideas and just talking about how clearly or well I have presented them. Reply to my text as a human, not as a helper, teacher, evaluator, or coach." When you ask for a reply, you are really inviting your listeners to enter into a discussion with you about the topic. You are thus also inviting them to leave your writing behind as they get involved in the issues themselves. Nevertheless, such a discussion can be one of the most helpful things of all for your writing. Since you are inviting a discussion, you should feel free to jump in and take full part. For this kind of feedback, you don't need to hold back and mostly listen.

<u>Reply</u> for "What's Wrong with Black English?": One Reader:

Dear Yoko,

Although I liked reading your essay, I want to argue against it. I have always considered Ebonics a type of slang, but now I'm not sure. Is it a real language? Does it follow a specific set of rules? Also, how is society hurting children's identity by not teaching Ebonics in schools? I agree with you that "children have the right to their own language," but it can be spoken at home, with friends, and in the neighborhood. The language will not die if it isn't taught in class. The arguments against bilingual education you use in the essay seem rather extreme to me. I feel like you have limited your options by so forcefully arguing for bilingual education. Perhaps your argument would be even stronger if you could mention more opposing arguments to bilingual education. This way, I would know you have at least considered them and then rejected them.

Another Reader:

• *All through my schooling, teachers corrected my mistakes in language. Especially in writing, but sometimes even in speaking. I'm white so they weren't "black" mistakes. They were just "mistakes." I've never thought that maybe I have a "right" to my mistakes. It sounds crazy, but*

Exploring the Writing Process

I spent a long time writing a good draft of a memo to teachers in the writing program. I was making suggestions for an evaluation process I wanted them to use. (I wanted them to write reflectively about their teaching and visit each other's classes.) I worked out a plan very carefully and at the end I really *wanted* them to do this—realizing of course that some would not want to. The more I thought about it, the more I felt I was right. I ended up putting it very strongly: They *have* to do it.

I read my draft out loud in a staff meeting to Pat, Bruce, Jeff, Aaron, and Cindy. Wanted feedback. People were slow to bring up that final bit (that they *have* to do it), but finally Cindy brought it up bluntly as a problem. Some disagreed and said, in effect, "Yes, we've got to insist." But Bruce and Jeff thought the way I wrote it went too far—would get readers' backs up unnecessarily. ("I don't want to be inflammatory," I said, and Aaron replied, "But you seem to want to make a flame.")

I wanted to defend what I wrote, but I held back; but the impulse to defend kept recurring. Finally I saw that I *could* make my point more mildly—and it would get my point across *more* effectively. I could

see it was better the milder way. Finally, I ended up feeling, "That's what I *wanted* to say."

I tell the story—it came to me this morning as I woke up early—as a paradigm of how feedback can and should work, of writing as a potentially collaborative social process. That is, it now strikes me that I *needed* to write those things; I needed to punch it to them. But by having the chance to read it out loud to this surrogate audience rather than the real one—an audience of peers with whom I felt safe—I could "get it said." And then listen; and finally hear.

By the end, I felt comfortable and grateful at the outcome—even though of course some little part of me still experienced it as having to "back down" and "accept criticism." Yet by the end, it didn't feel like backing down and "doing it their way." By the end it was what *I* wanted to say.

In short, the process of reading a draft to a safe audience and getting feedback wasn't just a way to "fix" my draft. The main thing was that *it allowed my mind to change.* My intention ended up being different from what it had been.

Peter Elbow

it's fun to think about. I never thought about all these corrections as hurting my cultural confidence, but they sure hurt my writing confidence. I grew up feeling dumb and feeling I could never have a job that required writing. I think I could have done better if teachers had respected my language more and not considered me dumb because I made so many mistakes.

<u>Reply</u> for "The Power of Sprinkles":
One Reader:

Dear Gabrielle,

I love your essay. I often talk out problems to myself also. I could relate to your confused feelings about writing. I can remember writing essays in high-school English classes and wondering if I should express my full opinions or be safe and write what I knew would receive an *A*. I have noticed since I've been at college, however, that professors encourage freedom in writing and creativity. This makes me think further about what high-school teachers want students to learn. By restricting students to follow a format, teachers are oppressing students' abilities. I really enjoyed the outcome of the dialogue when both of your voices agreed to challenge the teacher's expectations and write a creative essay.

Another Reader:

- It looked as though you were having fun with this. I enjoy reading it, but I'm jealous and actually it makes me mad. People like you could always get better grades with your creative tricks. I can't find ways to worm out of the actual assignment as it is spelled out. I do what I'm supposed to do, I work harder than you, and I always get a worse grade.

6. Voice

Voice is a large, rich concept that you can explore more fully in the workshop we devoted to it in Workshop 5. But to get feedback about voice you can ask two questions that get at two dimensions of voice in writing: (a) "How much voice do you hear in my writing? Is my language alive, human, resonant? Or is it dead, bureaucratic, silent, unsayable?" (b) "What kind of voice or voices do you hear in my writing? Timid? Confident? Sarcastic? Whispering? Shouting? Pleading?" There are some interesting variations on the second question: "What kind of person does my writing sound like?" Or "What kind of person do I become in my writing?" Or "What side of me does my writing bring out?" Keep in mind that there are often *several voices* intertwined in a piece of writing. If you listen closely, you may hear someone move back and forth between confidence and uncertainty, between sincerity and sarcasm. The writing may draw out the various sides of the writer. Multiple voices need not be a problem; we all have multiple voices. The issue is whether they work well together or get in each other's way. In the case of essays, it's important to ask, "Do you trust the voice or person you hear in my writing?"

Responses about the voice or voices in a piece of writing are remarkably interesting and useful. They go to the heart of what makes writing work for readers, since our response to writing is often shaped by our sense of what kind of voice we are hearing. And voice gets to the heart of how we as writers come up with words, because we often write best when we feel we are "giving voice" to our thoughts; and we often revise best when we sense that the voice doesn't sound right and change it to get closer to the voice we want. In short, our *ear* may be the most powerful organ we have for both reading and writing. But some readers need a bit of practice in learning to hear and describe the voices in writing.

Make sure, as always, that everyone's piece gets two readings—perhaps by having one straight read-through and then a second reading for response.

Feedback about voice lends itself particularly to what is one of the most useful forms of feedback: rendering or enacting your words. You might get a listener to do your second reading, or even two listeners to do both readings. Or get listeners to read short bits where they hear a voice. It's interesting and fun to ask readers to bring out the voice or voices as they read. They'll have an easier time if you are willing to invite them to exaggerate or play around a bit: to read it as if they were whining or arrogant or depressed, or whatever the voice suggests to them. This can lead to some parody and silliness, so you mustn't take offense. The goal is to help you hear the various voices and potential voices in your words. If you are willing to invite this kind of performance, it will become the most lively and enjoyable of all forms of feedback.

SAMPLES OF FEEDBACK: VOICE

<u>Voice</u> for "What's Wrong with Black English?":
One Reader:

- Your voice starts out relaxed, friendly, and casual and then gets more authoritative as you start arguing by giving citations and examples to support your claims. This makes it sound like a research essay written for a tough class. Then at the end your voice gets back to the more relaxed tone it had in the beginning.

Another Reader:

- The tone of the voice in your paper is strong, assured, and confident. It seems it would be impossible to sway you in any other direction—you seem absolutely convinced about your argument. It almost comes across as stubborn. Your voice is sincere and even passionate about the topic—almost devoted to proving to your audience that you are right. I don't hear any trace of wondering or doubt in your voice.

<u>Voice</u> for "The Power of Sprinkles":
One Reader:

- The whole essay is in quotes and uses a lot of "*I.*" It's all in an out loud voice—like speaking more than like writing. The writer is frustrated and annoyed toward writing essays and is arguing with herself. The voice is very strong and challenging as the author is arguing.

Another Reader:

- The voice that doesn't want to write the essay is always changing: whining, arguing, thinking of clever points, being angry, making jokes. The voice that says you have to write the essay always has an answer; in the end it's a little smarter or a little better at handling the troublemaker voice. It's like the mommy who knows how to handle the quick-thinking rebellious child. It's just like a mommy to avoid an all-out fight and to use ice-cream as a bribe.

7. Movies of the Reader's Mind

What we need most as writers is not evaluation of the quality of our writing or advice about how to fix it, but an accurate account of what goes on inside readers' heads as they read our words. We need to learn to *feel* those readers on the other end of our line. When are they with us? When are they resisting? What kind of resistance is it—disagreement or annoyance? When are their minds wandering?

Movies of the reader's mind is the form of response that really underlies all other forms—the foundation of all feedback. After all, everything anyone might say about a text grows out of some reaction. Suppose, for example, that someone reads your essay and says she doesn't agree with your main point or doesn't like your voice in this piece. You need to ask her to back up and give you the movies of her mind that led to this conclusion: What did she understand your main point or your voice to be? Her movies may reveal to you that she doesn't disagree with you or dislike the voice; she *misunderstood* them. Therefore the cure (if you decide you want to adjust the piece for this reader) would not be to change your point or your voice but to make them stronger so that they are not misunderstood.

It's not so easy to give good movies of the mind. For example, a reader might tell you he feels your tone is too aggressive and wants you to soften it. But what were his *reactions*—the movies of his mind—that led to this reaction? Perhaps at first he can't tell you. ("I don't know. I was just bothered; that's all.") But if you ask him to ferret out those too-quick-to-notice reactions behind that conclusion, he might tell you that he felt irritated by what he thought were some sly digs you were making about people you disagree with. Once you learn what was actually happening in this reader, you can draw your own conclusions instead of having to buy or resist his. After getting back to his reactions, you may decide that the problem was not the "digs" themselves but the slyness. You might well decide that the solution you need is not to remove or soften what he felt as sly digs but to make your disagreement with others much more frank and blunt.

Movies of a reader's mind can be confusing until you are used to them. They consist of nothing but facts or raw data, not conclusions; and the same piece of writing causes different things to happen in different minds. What you get is messy. But movies gradually help you develop your sensitivity to what your words are likely to do inside readers' minds.

Movies do not require experts. Indeed, sometimes you get wonderfully clear and helpful movies from children or very naive readers. Sometimes sophisticated readers have a hard time getting behind their judgments and conclusions to the feelings and reactions that led to them. You need honesty and trust.

Here are some ways to help readers learn to notice and describe their reactions while reading:

• *Serialize or interrupt your text.* Read your writing to listeners one section at a time (or hand them your text one section at a time). At each interruption, get them to tell you what's going on in their heads right at that moment. These "stop-frame movies" are particularly important near the beginning of your piece so that you can find out how your opening affects readers. In particular, you need to know whether your opening has made them resist you or go along with you. That is, readers' reactions to the rest of your piece often depend on whether they became friendly or unfriendly during the first few paragraphs. For the rest of your piece, either they are pedaling with you and helping you along or they are dragging their heels and seeing every possible problem. If you give them a written version of your piece to read at home, persuade them to interrupt their reading at least two or three times and take a few notes of what's actually happening in their minds at the time of each interruption. This technique helps them capture their reactions "on the fly."

- *Get their responses in story form.*   Get readers to tell you their responses in the form of a story; that is, "First I felt this, then I thought that," and so on. The story form prevents them from falling into useless global generalities like "I enjoyed it" or "It was exciting" or "I was bored."

- *Get "I-statements."*   If a reader says, "You should change this word or move that paragraph," you don't know what was happening to him: Was he bored, confused, or in disagreement? Get readers to tell their reactions in sentences starting with "I."

We have held off movies of the reader's mind until now—until you've tried other kinds of feedback and, we hope, developed trust in yourself and a relationship of trust and support with your readers—because movies are not always easy to listen to. If readers tell you honestly what went on as they were reading your words, you may well hear something like, "I was getting madder and madder because I felt lost—starting in the first paragraph. And I felt your voice was arrogant too, and so I wanted to quarrel with everything, even when I agreed with your actual points." It's hard to benefit from responses like that unless you feel them coming from a friend or ally.

When a reader gives you movies of reactions that are very critical, remember that she is not trying to be fair or impartial (as in "evaluating by criteria," which comes later in our sequence). She is just trying to tell you accurately what was occurring in her. She is not pretending to be God making an objective judgment. These are simply her subjective reactions, and they might be different from those of most other readers.

Here are some other suggestions for getting movies of readers' minds:

- Don't make apologies or explanations of your writing before they hear or read it and respond, because these will heavily influence how they react.

- Don't quarrel with what a reader says, even if he's utterly misunderstanding what you wrote. You're not trying to educate readers about your text; you're trying to get *them* to educate *you* about your text.

- Invite exaggeration or parody. This can be scary, but also a big help if your readers are having trouble telling you what's happening as they read or if they seem to be beating around the bush. For example, readers might feel vaguely bothered by something in your writing but be unable to explain what they feel. "It's OK," they'll say. "I pretty much liked what you wrote." But you can feel some hesitation or reservation. If you feel brave enough to invite them to exaggerate their reaction, they will often find words for what's going on and say something like this: "If I were to exaggerate, I'd say you are beating me over the head here." You need to feel fairly secure before you ask for exaggeration because it may lead to a strong statement. But an element of play or humor can keep things from getting too sticky. For example, another helpful question is this: "What would a *parody* of my paper look like?" They might then reply: "Well, I guess it would be a three-page soapbox rant that's all one breathless sentence." You can reassure them that you know this is not an accurate or fair picture of your piece, but this distorted picture captures a *tendency* in your piece.

- Movies of the mind requires honesty from readers and reveals as much about them as about your writing. If you aren't getting honesty, perhaps you haven't convinced your readers that you really want it.

SAMPLES OF FEEDBACK: MOVIES OF THE READER'S MIND

<u>Movies of the Reader's Mind</u> for "What's Wrong with Black English?": One Reader:

- When she said that some Japanese liked the fashion of blacks, it reminded me of my friend in Singapore who liked rap music so much that he was willing to pay high prices for it.
- Isn't "African-American" more acceptable than "Black"?
- I could not see the link between music and English when she was talking about blacks attracting people and then suddenly moved to the debate about language among educators.
- I felt that the tone was authoritative when she said that black children "should" be taught in both Black English and Standard English. But I didn't quite agree with the point, as it is not easy to master two kinds of English simultaneously.
- I could see images of minds of confused and disappointed black children when they are told that their culture is not accepted in the public.
- I felt the quotation made a very good point—that the schools have to change, not the children.
- I felt that the statement, "You cannot abandon language just because it is spoken by poor people," has a lot of meaning. It brought the title of the essay back into my mind.
- I completely agree that language is culture. It reminded me of another class I'm taking (about the interpretation of meaning) where that was exactly what I have argued.
- I definitely agree that in today's society, power exists in Standard English, and I can see the importance for black children of learning Standard English as well.
- At the end I get reminded of the introduction as she addresses the Japanese liking of American culture because of its diversity. But in my mind I actually doubted that.

Another Reader:

- The first paragraph grabbed my attention immediately. The writer talks about African-American cultural influence in Japan. The writer, being Japanese herself, gives an insider's view, and she goes on talking about personal observations which intrigued me even more. I wanted to hear more about American black culture and how other cultures imitate it. I wondered how else "blacks of America and their culture have the power of attracting people." I am eager to hear more.

Note: Our normal method of collaborating on the first edition was for one of us to start a unit—do a very rough draft—and give it to the other to work on. The second person would just take it over—make it his or hers, make extensive changes—especially because the first version was often still quite un-formed. Then what the second person pro-duced would go back to the first person for more revision. All this usually on disks rather than on paper.

In this way we often lost track of who started something and who "owned" a sec-tion or an idea. We pretty much drifted or fell into this method: we were in a hurry, we knew we had a lot to write, and we didn't have time or energy to "protect" everything we wrote. Most of all we trusted each other. It worked remarkably well.

But for this particular unit we proceeded differently. Peter had worked out a fairly full outline and I took on the job of writing a draft from that outline. Then, instead of Peter taking it over from there—as we nor-mally did—he wrote marginal feedback and gave it back to me to revise. Thus we drifted into a problematic arrangement for this unit: I was writing a unit which felt like Peter's—and getting feedback from him about how to revise what I'd written.

I'm revising according to feedback and angry. Why doesn't he write the damn thing himself if he knows so surely what he wants? It's insulting—giving it back to me to do *his* way. I can't do it. I feel as though I'm not into it, not into the ideas—just into superficial stuff, trying to make it what someone else wants it to be. I'd like to just give it back to him and say that: "Here, you have such a sure idea about what this should be, why give it to me to do? I'm not a typist." Does he think I'm inept? stupid? Maybe he's right. Maybe I'm no good at this and he's saying these things so he won't have to say that. He doesn't think "Life is unfair" is good. But I like it and I'll keep it.

He wants this to be mainly a paper handed in to a professor in some other class, not an explanation for the self of something difficult. But I prefer the latter. So I kept trying to make the unit into what he wanted, while still thinking my idea was good.

But somehow (because he's a nice guy I guess) I kept on working with the suggestions. And as I wrote, I got caught up in thinking about getting stu-dents to see something two different ways: for them-selves and for others. An interesting problem pre-sented itself to me for solution. Could I make it work out that way? I began to explore, and suddenly it was *my* idea; although it wasn't suddenly—just my real-ization of what had happened seemed sudden. Apparently I was writing according to the feedback, and the idea became mine. I saw an interesting way to develop it, potential for the unit I hadn't seen be-fore, ideas I had never written before. I got excited about it because it was good. Then I could write again without anger or resistance.

The feedback was gone; I really didn't look at any more of the marginal comments because they no longer mattered. I had my own way to go. I just for-got the way it had been done. When I finished up and polished it a bit, I looked back and who'd be-lieve it! I had, on my own, come to saying almost ex-actly the same thing he said later on in the part of the feedback I hadn't even read. That's eerie! This must be an instance of authentically situated voice— somehow using the words and ideas of others and forging them in the furnace of my own word hoard. The ideas I got caught up with seemed to begin to write themselves out. But they also produced an in-teresting intellectual challenge to me. And there was something very satisfying about discovering that the two of us had been on the same wavelength—or close anyhow. His good ideas had fertilized my good ideas, and we ended up with something that was un-doubtedly better than anything either of us could have done alone. It has been worth working through the anger.

Pat Belanoff

- In the second paragraph, I am beginning to disagree with the writer when she says that banning Black English only hurts children's identity and is a public rejection of their culture and language. Because this is my first disagreement, I notice myself doubting the writer more.
- As I read the third paragraph, I become confused. I don't understand the author's reasoning. How can public separation be brought about by a culture feeling shame because of their poverty? The writer argues that instilling pride in the next generation of blacks (teaching them Ebonics in school) will help them climb the socioeconomic ladder. Now I am lost again when the writer says America will view blacks differently when the majority of them become middle class—and the way they become middle class is through learning Ebonics. Why will it change the view of blacks in America? How will it change the view?
- As I read the fourth paragraph, I feel offended when I get to the point that "Standard English and an understanding of white middle class rules and codes are necessary tools for social success." This upset me. I never realized that middle-class rules and codes set by the middle class ensure success. However, I suppose I felt offended because I am white and middle class. I think I would have felt better if she broadened her view by at least bringing in arguments criticizing bilingual education. She can still reject them, but I would have felt more place for my views and feelings.
- As a read back over it all, I feel unsettled. I still resist but I see I have to think more and find out more. It wasn't till I read back over it more carefully that I realized that she said clearly that she was arguing for also teaching Standard English to black students.

Yet Another Reader:

- The first time I read "What's Wrong with Black English?" was by accident. I was flipping through the 1997–1998 Writing Program anthology and just happened upon it. The title caught my eye instantly. Then I read it. It felt racy and I liked how it expressed racial issues bluntly; I'd never heard anything like this before. Most of this piece was admonishing whites and teachers for believing "Black English" was incorrect. I was raised to believe that was true. I liked that Ms. Koga used opposing view points in her argument; it shows the other side of this issue.

<u>Movies of a Reader's Mind</u> for "The Power of Sprinkles":
One Reader:

- What is going on? was my first reaction, and then it all became very clear.
- I felt that the repetition of "I don't want to do this" conveyed a strong force of feelings.
- I could picture the two sides of a person's mind debating over what should be done.
- I could relate to almost everything the author talks about, as these are all common, everyday things that all college students do.
- I felt that there is little chance of disagreement with the essay since both sides of everything mentioned is presented almost immediately.
- I found the essay fun to read as I was getting involved by taking one side of the author's mind and trying to see if my arguments are being countered. I felt as though I were arguing with my own mind.
- When the author said "because this is assigned!" I was saying to myself, Exactly! and thus I agree that something we are told to do by a specific deadline is different than deciding to do something by ourself.
- I got a little bored at the part about "making an essay longer or shorter"—since I don't feel problems about that.
- The "green eggs and ham" things reminded me of the fiction essay I wrote, and I agree that it was fun.
- The ending made me smile and reflect back to the title. Till then I didn't think about the title. I suddenly felt that the author thought of the title only after completing the essay.

Another Reader:

- As I read the first part of the paper, I automatically associate myself with the writer since she is addressing an issue I deal with as well (as a student). Therefore I automatically have trust in the writer and am interested in reading the rest of the essay. As I read and the two voices continue to fight about writing the assigment, I begin to hear the argument in my head and I notice myself emphasizing the words. When there is an exclamation point, I read the sentence with energy and emphasis.

  As I read further into the paper, I only become more involved and more supportive of voice one. The voices converse with each other about teachers who attach so many limitations on writing that it isn't fun. While reading, bad memories came to my mind of high-school days when I had to conform to the writing teacher's requirements. I, too, would get back essays that I labored over saying it didn't meet the length requirement, and the score would drop one letter grade. I can relate to the frustrations of voice one. I was proud of the voices at the end of the essay when they decided to write how and what they wanted. The voices valued freedom in writing more than following rules. I felt really positive when I finished reading the essay. I thought to myself, She's right, you can beat the system if you're clever!

8. Metaphorical Descriptions

It turns out that you can usually see a faint star better out of the corner of your eye than when you look at it directly. The same thing happens in the middle of the night when you try to see the faint luminous dial of the bedside clock: a squint from the corner of your eye usually shows you more. So too, we can often capture more of what we know about something if we talk *indirectly*—through metaphor—than if we try to say directly what we see. For metaphorical feedback, get readers to describe what you have written in some of the following terms:

Weather(s). What is the weather of the writing? sunny? drizzling? foggy? Try noticing different weathers in different parts of the writing.

Clothing. How has the writer "dressed" what he has to say? In faded denims? In formal dinner wear? In a carefully chosen torn T-shirt?

Shape. Picture the shape of the piece—perhaps even in a drawing.

Color(s). If the writing were a color, what would it be? Different colors at different spots?

Animal(s). Ditto.

Writer-to-reader relationship. Draw a picture or tell a story with the writer and the reader in it. See what kind of relationship seems to get implied between writer and reader.

To give metaphorical feedback, you must enter into the game. Don't strain or struggle for answers: just relax and say the answers that come to mind, even if you don't understand them or know why they come to mind. Some of the answers may be "off the wall," and some of the good ones will seem so. Just give answers and trust the connections your mind comes up with.

The writer, too, must listen in the same spirit of play: listen and accept and not struggle to figure out what these answers mean. The writer, like the responder, needs to trust that there is useful material in there, even if it's mixed with things that aren't so useful. An owl swallows a mouse whole and trusts her innards to sort out what is useful and what's not. You too can eat like an owl: Listen in an attitude of trust that your mind will use what makes sense and ignore what does not.

There's a side benefit to this kind of feedback. It highlights an important truth for almost all feedback: that we are not looking for "right answers." We're looking for individual perceptions—ways of seeing. And it all works best if there is a spirit of play and trust.

SAMPLES OF FEEDBACK: METAPHORICAL DESCRIPTIONS

<u>Metaphorical Descriptions</u> for "What's Wrong with Black English?":
One Reader:

- This essay reminds me of a fast moving thunderstorm. It starts off as dark clouds on the horizon. Then the patter of rain begins. Suddenly the wind picks up and lightning splits the sky. The soft sound of rain is transformed into hard pellets as it punishes the earth, slamming into the ground. But just as quickly as it came, the storm passes. The roiling clouds move on to reveal the sun glinting off the newly wetted earth.
- Shape. Polygon.
- Animal. Squirrel.

Another Reader:

- If the essay were an item of clothing, it would be a brand new pair of jeans that don't quite fit right and that have a few holes that weren't apparent at the department store when the jeans were bought.
- If the essay were a type of weather, it would begin as a sunny day which then turns into fog with scattered rain showers.
- If the essay were an animal, it would be a mischievous cat.
- If the essay were a shape, it would be a hexagon.

<u>Metaphorical Descriptions</u> for "The Power of Sprinkles":
One Reader:

- If the essay were an item of clothing, it would be a reversible, warm, colorful down coat with lots of hidden pockets for gum and Chapstick.
- If the essay were weather, it would be a refreshing cool sprinkle on a hot, sticky, humid day.
- If the essay were an animal, it would be a monkey.
- If the essay were a color, it would be chartreuse.
- If the essay were a shape, it would be a diamond.

Another Reader:

- Weather. It's like thunder and lightning at the beginning during the argument and it calms down to the smooth waves of the sea at the end.
- Clothing. Plain T-shirt and shorts.
- Shape. Triangle.
- Color. Light green.
- Animal. Mongoose.
- Picture of the writer-to-reader relationship. It's as if the author is constantly talking to me, but actually ignoring me because she is arguing with herself.

9. Believing and Doubting

This kind of response zeros in on the content or ideas in your writing. It invariably gives you more ideas, more material. The obvious place to use it is on essays, but if you ask readers to play the believing and doubting game with your stories, you'll get interesting feedback too.

Believing

Simply ask readers to believe everything you have written, and then tell you what they notice as a result of believing. Even if they disagree strongly with what you have written, their job is to *pretend* to agree. In this way, they will act as your ally: They can give you more reasons or evidence for what you have written; they can give you different and better ways of thinking about your topic.

Doubting

Now ask readers to pretend that everything you've written is false—to find as many reasons as they can why you are wrong in what you say (or why your story doesn't make sense).

Here are some techniques that help with doubting and believing:

- *Role-play.* Instead of being yourself, pretend to be someone else who *does* believe or doubt the piece, and think of the things this person would see and say. It's a game; just pretend.

Exploring the Writing Process

Why can't I deal with this? The feedback from both of them is enormously useful, but it makes me uncomfortable and mad. I'm all stirred up. It leaves me upset and unable to sleep or relax. I think the crucial factor is that it doesn't feel like it's coming from an ally. I feel I have to fight. That's the main response: Wanting to fight them. Energized for fight. Aggression. Unable to relax. Unable to put it aside. Caught.

I guess you could call that useful. It certainly triggers a piece of my character that is strong. I'm a fighter. My intellectual life is, in a way, a fight. (Perhaps I should talk about this in the Believing essay. I'm in combat.) But it's so exhausting always to be in combat. Yes, it is energizing; it keeps one going. But is it really the best way to go? I wonder if it brings out the *best* thinking. Thinking with my dukes up too much?

Compare the effect of this feedback with the effect of the feedback I got from Paul on the same draft. It was so energizing and comforting. But not sleepy comforting. It made me go back to my thoughts and ideas. It got me *unstuck* from the adversarial defensive mode where I'm trying to beat these guys. It sent me back into my thoughts and simply had me explore what I had to say.

The comparison casts an interesting light on the public and private dimensions of writing. Feedback from _____ and _____ keeps me fixated on *them*—on audience. I want to beat them. Paul's feedback sends me back into myself and helps me forget about audience.

Peter Elbow

- Imagine a different world where everything that the piece says is true (or false): Enter into that make-believe world and tell what you see. Or tell the story of what a world would be like where everything that the piece says is true (or false).

Usually it makes the most sense to start with the believing game. So first, ask your readers to find all the possibilities and richness in what you have written: build it up before tearing it down. But if readers have trouble believing, they might need to start with the doubting game. This can get the doubting out of their system or satisfy that skeptical itch, and afterward they might find themselves freer to enter into a way of thinking that is foreign to them.

You don't necessarily need to get both kinds of feedback. If you are working on an early draft—or you feel very fragile about something you have written—it can be very useful to get *only* believing responses. This is a way to ask people frankly to support and help you in making your case or imagining the world you are trying to describe. Conversely, if you have a late draft that you feel confident about and are trying to prepare for a tough audience, you might ask only for doubting.

Readers will benefit from a spirit of play in giving this kind of response, and you will, too, as a writer, especially when you are listening to the doubting response. People can get carried away with the skeptical wet-blanket game. (School trains us to doubt, not to believe.) You might hear lots of reasons why what you wrote is wrong. Taken as a game, doubting needn't bother you. What's more, this play dimension helps you take all feedback in the right spirit. For feedback is nothing but help in trying to see what you have written through various lenses—to see what you can't see with your lens.

SAMPLES OF FEEDBACK: BELIEVING AND DOUBTING

<u>Believing</u> for "What's Wrong with Black English?":
One Reader:

- Children should be proud of their own language. They can't be expected to speak a different language in the school and a different language at home while thinking that the latter is inferior. Schools should see that Black English is popular not only in the U.S. but also in other countries and should teach it. Students can't use language well if they are ashamed of their real language. Teachers would be more successful in helping all students have confidence and enjoy reading and writing if they learned to honor Black English.

Another Reader:

- A predominantly white middle class is oppressing the cultures of the poor, or anyone different. The white middle class is afraid of the coming of values from a different culture, they persecute it; they don't want a shift in power.
- Language is culture. All should be taught in our public schools. The country will be stronger when we can benefit from all citizens and all cultures.
- The English language is actually already a mixture of all kinds of different languages, slangs, and dialects. That's what makes it a rich language. Honoring Black English will eventually make Standard English more vibrant.
- Some of the best contributions to U.S. music have come from black culture, especially jazz and much popular music. The same thing can happen with language. Black language is turning up in literature.
- We'll see that the concept of "standard language" is a problem, and just talk instead about "good and effective language."

- Black students will be able to help white students understand language better because they'll have two languages and be good at switching, especially when this switching happens as part of school, not as a hidden process.

<u>Believing</u> for "The Power of Sprinkles":
One Reader:

- There is a sense of nobleness in challenging people's expectations of you.
- Writing is fun. We can make jokes even with what is unpleasant.
- If you avoid the straightforward path, things will be easier and more fun.

Another Reader:

- We all argue with ourselves like this.
- There is no "I"—only a "we." We are nothing but a collection of shifting voices.
- Writing is usually a struggle, but there are always ways around the struggle. If we really talk to ourselves honestly, we can find a way to handle things.
- Life is essentially a playful game.

<u>Doubting</u> for "What's Wrong with Black English?":
One Reader:

- Black students will benefit more from having to use Standard English in schools. Teachers can help black students use Standard English and still not put them down or make them feel that there is something wrong with them or their language. And black students can still use their own language at home and with friends.
- Another language in our crappy school system would overtax our resources.
- Standard English will be enriched better by Black English if black students have to use it.

Another Reader:

- Well, when you speak of Japan, how many people in Japan enjoy Black English? And that has nothing to do with the schools in the U.S. not teaching Black English. How is it possible to teach both forms of English in one school when there are white students also in the classes? And even if they did teach both forms of English, how would it be fair for black children to have to learn both the languages and still cope with their other school work while the white students have less burden?
- A single unifying language is necessary for any country to be whole. America was based on the idea of a ruling middle class. It just happens that a significant portion of the middle class is white. I know many African-American middle-class people, and most of them do not use Black English. Your assumption that Standard English is white is incorrect. Standard English is just middle class in accordance with the values that our society holds.

<u>Doubting</u> for "The Power of Sprinkles":
One Reader:

- You can't just write anything silly and claim that you have written an essay. An essay should spell out your thoughts, and they must be carefully crafted and properly refined in order to make a good essay.
- Why do you have to wait till the last minute to do your homework—until when your friends are watching a movie? How can you concentrate on the essay this way?

Another Reader:

- Not everyone has problems writing.
- Are you schizophrenic?
- Planning time to do your homework might help; it makes things easier.

10. Skeleton Feedback and Descriptive Outline

In literature classes we tend to describe what is going on in a story, poem, or novel, rather than judge it or find mistakes. Inherent in such an approach is *respect for the text,* and the response is a way to see the text better, allowing the text to speak on its own. You will benefit from asking for the same kind of respect for your writing, and from showing that kind of respect to the writing of others. We suggest here two ways for describing a text.

Skeleton Feedback

A good way to analyze the reasoning and the structure in almost any essay is to get readers to answer the following questions:

- What do you see as the main point/claim/assertion of the whole paper?
- What are the main reasons or subsidiary points? It's fine to list them as they come—in any order.
- Taking each reason in turn, what support or evidence or examples are given—or could be given—for it?
- What assumptions does the paper seem to make about the topic or issue? That is, what does the essay take for granted?
- What assumptions does the paper seem to make about the audience? Who or what kinds of readers does the writer seem to be talking to (and how are they most likely to react to the ideas in the paper)? How does the writer seem to treat the readers? as enemies? friends? children? In short, what is the writer's stance toward the audience?
- Finally, what suggestions do you have? About the order or organization? About things to add or drop or change?

It probably makes the most sense for readers to answer these questions in writing and at leisure—with the text in hand. However, you could get this kind of feedback orally if you have a group that will cooperate in working out shared answers to the questions.

Descriptive Outline

This procedure (developed by Kenneth Bruffee) involves a sustained process of analyzing the *meaning* and *function* of discourse. You can't really do a descriptive outline unless you have the text in hand and take time: This is a kind of feedback that needs to be written.

The procedure is to write a *says* sentence and a *does* sentence for each paragraph or section, and then for the whole essay. A *says* sentence summarizes the meaning or message. A *does* sentence describes the function—what the paragraph or piece is trying to do or accomplish with readers (for example, "This paragraph introduces the topic of the essay by means of a humorous anecdote" or "This paragraph brings up an objection that some readers might feel, and then tries to answer that objection").

The key to writing *does* sentences is to keep them different from the *says* sentences. Keep them from even mentioning the content of the paragraph. Thus, you shouldn't be able to tell from a *does* sentence whether the paragraph is talking about cars or ice cream. Here is a *does* sentence that slides into being a *says* sentence: "This paragraph gives an example of how women's liberation has affected men more than it has women." To make it a real *does* sentence, remove any mention of the ideas or content and talk only about function: "This paragraph gives an example" would do. Or perhaps better, "This paragraph gives an example designed to surprise the reader."

The power in both skeleton feedback and descriptive outlines comes from the distance and detachment they provide. Thus, they are useful for *giving yourself* feedback—particularly when you feel all tangled or caught up in your piece from having worked long and closely on it.

SAMPLES OF FEEDBACK: SKELETON FEEDBACK AND DESCRIPTIVE OUTLINE

<u>Skeleton Feedback</u> for "What's Wrong with Black English?": One Reader:

Main point:
- Allowing black children to be taught in Black English will give them cultural confidence which will in turn help them rise in society.

Other points and support:
- Blacks of America are influential worldwide.
  —Writer's experience in Japan.
- Forcing black children to learn in English is hurting their identity.
  —They see their culture is rejected in public.
  —Also, the quotation from Delpit.
- Speaking a language felt as lower class makes people feel ashamed of themselves and causes public separation of groups.
  —Supported by a quotation from Rodriguez.
  —But the writer doesn't agree with this point.
- Language keeps culture alive.
  —Appeal to common sense. I don't see others supporting this point.
- White middle-class rules and codes are necessary for success.
  —Appeal to common sense. I don't see others supporting this point.
- The United States is admired for its diversity.
  —Appeal to history and national pride.

Assumptions:
- Ebonics is a language.
- Public separation is due to cultural groups feeling inadequate.
- When the majority of blacks become middle class, America's whole way of thinking will change.
- Opponents of bilingual teaching trying to put blacks down.
- The audience is knowledgeable about Ebonics.

Assumptions about audience:

• The writer seems to treat us in a friendly open way. She is strongly sincere in her argument, but she seems to assume that we will agree with her when she gives her reasons. She's using reason and quiet emotion. Even though she's making an argument, I feel she would be surprised that I am still resisting her.

Suggestions:

• Spend more time understanding and dealing with resisting arguments. I'm confused at her wording in her use of the first quotation. Give me some examples or stories of how this is actually needed or would actually work.

Skeleton Feedback for "The Power of Sprinkles":
One Reader:

Main point:

• Writing doesn't need guidelines and it doesn't have to be formal to be a good, solid, effective piece of work.

Other points:

• Teachers discourage writers from expressing sincere opinions by forcing them to write about topics which they hold no interest in.
• Teachers discourage freedom in writing by setting length limits and maximums.
• The writer only enjoys writing when on a daily basis for fun and writing for a class should not be different.
• Personal satisfaction is much greater when one is allowed to write creatively, the way she wants.

Assumptions about audience:

• The writer assumes we can get along without any explanations of what's happening. She assumes we'll go along with the playfulness and not worry that we don't know till the end what the title means.

Suggestions:

• I can't think of any suggestions. It works so well.

Another Reader:

Main point:

• We can get this paper written if we learn to talk to each other, listen to each other, and work together.

Other points:

• I don't want to write.
• There are positive aspects of writing. You write every day. Writing skills are essential for communication in life (e-mail, memos, lists, directions, notes, letters, journals, etc.).
• Yes, but such daily writing rituals are fun because I am free to say what I want and at whatever length I want. Why do teachers ask us to add more to papers, when they are only asking for extended "bull_ _ _ _." I'm not free to express my true opinions due to fear of getting my grade docked by a disagreeing teacher.
• Sometimes I can be unique and creative even on school assignments. Sometimes when I do what I want instead of what I am told, the finished product is better. I can add humor and silliness to papers and the quality improves.
• Let's work together and do it just this once—and give ourselves a treat for a reward.

Descriptive Outline for "What's Wrong with Black English?":
One Reader:

- Says, essay as a whole: Black English is necessary in the classroom in order for poor blacks to improve their position in society.
- Does, essay as a whole: Does present an argument.
- Says, first paragraph: Blacks are admired worldwide; their culture will die or suffer if their "language" is not used in school.
- Does, first paragraph: Gives an observation or example from a great distance—and doesn't even bring up the issue of the essay.
- Says, second paragraph: Schools need to foster black pride in African-American children.
- Does, second paragraph: Moves to U.S. and brings up main topic; summarizes and argues her position; adds quotation for support.
- Says, third paragraph: Some people think that children who don't speak Standard English will be helped by being made to use it in school, but that isn't the way to help them.
- Does, third paragraph: Gives an opposing argument and answers it.
- Says, fourth paragraph: Black children need to be taught Standard English too in order to be successful in society.
- Does, fourth paragraph: Emphasizes that the writer is not arguing an "either/or" position but a "both/and" position.
- Says, final paragraph: The strength and spirit of America have come from its acceptance of many cultures.
- Does, fifth paragraph: Summarizes and concludes by appealing to history and national pride.

Note: A descriptive outline isn't appropriate for a playful and indirect dialogue like "The Power of Sprinkles."

11. Criterion-Based Feedback

You may well have been getting a bit of this kind of feedback all along. No matter what kind of response you are asking for, it's hard not to ask your readers a few questions about aspects of your writing you feel uncertain about. "I've been trying to get this complicated piece clearly organized and easy to follow. Have I succeeded for you?" "I've done a lot of cutting. Does it feel too choppy?" "I want this to be fun to read, not a chore. Have I succeeded with you?"

The piece of writing itself will suggest certain of its own criteria, usually depending on function. For example, the main job might be to *convey information.* Or, as the writer, you can specify the criteria you consider most important, for example, tone or voice.

Criteria for Nonfiction Writing

The criteria traditionally applied to essays or nonfiction or expository writing are these:

- *Focus on task.* If the piece is written in response to an assignment, question, or task, does it squarely *address* it?
- *Content.* Are there good ideas, interesting or original insights? Are the ideas supported with reasons, evidence, examples?
- *Organization.* It's important to realize that even unconventional organization can be successful. The *real* questions about organization are always these: Does the *beginning* serve as a good way to bring readers in? Do the *middle parts* lead readers successfully where they need to go? Does the *ending* give a satisfying sense of completion or closure? Notice, for example, that many successful essays begin with an anecdote or example such that readers don't even know what the essay will be about, much less what it will be saying. The opening is successful because the anecdote works to get readers involved so that they don't mind not knowing where they are going.
- *Coherence among sentences.* Do sentences seem to follow satisfactorily from each other?
- *Clarity of language.*
- *Voice.* What is the voice or persona and the stance toward the reader, and do they work well?
- *Mechanics.* Spelling, grammar, punctuation; proofreading.

Criteria for Fiction Writing

The criteria that are traditionally applied to imaginative writing, such as fiction or narrative, are these:

- *Plot.* Is it a believable, interesting, or meaningful story?
- *Character.* Do we find characters real or interesting?
- *Description, vividness of details.* Do we *experience* what's there?
- *Language.* Not just "Is it clear?" but "Is it alive and resonant with meaning—perhaps through imagery and metaphor?"
- *Meaning; "So what?"* Is there a meaning or impact that makes the piece seem important or resonant?

Specifying Criteria Helps in Giving Feedback to Yourself

Criteria give you a kind of leverage or perspective, and help focus your attention on things you might otherwise miss when you read over what you've written. Before reading over a draft, you can pause and consciously ask yourself, "What criteria are the most important for this piece of writing?" or "What features of writing do I especially need to be careful about?" This will help you see more.

To Readers

You can make your criterion-based responses more valuable in two ways:

- Be specific: point to particular passages and words which lead you to the judgments you make.

- Be honest and try to give the writer the movies of your mind that lie behind these judgments. That is, what *reactions in you* led to these judgments? For example, if you felt the organization was poor, were you actually feeling lost as you read, or just somewhat distracted or merely disapproving?

SAMPLES OF FEEDBACK: CRITERION-BASED FEEDBACK

<u>Criterion-Based Feedback</u> for "What's Wrong with Black English?": One Reader:

- Clarity of sentences and ideas: I found it smooth to read, easy to follow. But I felt a bit confused in her use of the quotation at the end of the second paragraph.
- Voice: I found it ambitious, honest, quietly strong, confident.
- Ability to convince: For me, more explanations were needed and the original ideas need to be expanded.
- Techniques for arguing: a lot.
    - She used a novel approach by coming at a U.S. debate from a Japanese point of view.
    - She acknowledged an opposing argument, but only one.
    - She used quotations from published authors on both sides of the issue.
    - She appealed to history and national pride.
    - She tried to show how her position is not really one-sided.

<u>Criterion-Based Feedback</u> for "The Power of Sprinkles": One Reader:

- Style: Very creative.
- Clarity: The argument was easy to understand.
- Voice: Informal language used, but it is a personal conversation and would only be appropriate in such context.
- Tone: Sincere and yet also ironic and witty.
- Ability to convince: The voices gave good arguments and examples.
- Ability to throw light on the psychology of writing and dealing with assignment: Hearing two voices got at the complexity of inner struggle.

Final Word: Taking Charge of the Feedback Process by Choosing among These Techniques

We want to end by emphasizing the main point here: As writer, you need to take charge of the process of getting feedback on your work. We've created what could be called an artificial anatomy of *kinds* of feedback in order to help you take charge. For if you simply ask someone to give you feedback or response to what you've written and don't give any help or direction, they will probably just imitate the responses they remember getting from teachers. With the best will in the world, they will probably try to find things that are wrong or weak and then try to tell you how to fix them. Yet they are likely to do this badly: They may well call something wrong or weak in your writing that is in fact just fine. And even if they do it well, this may not be the kind of response that will help you most given your temperament and where you are with this piece.

Now that you've tried out these kinds of feedback—both getting them and giving them—you will be better at knowing what kind of feedback would help you most, and better at helping someone give it to you. And if you want feedback from someone outside your class who hasn't practiced these techniques, you can just show them samples in this book and they will get a pretty clear idea of what you are asking for.

Sometimes when you have a trusted reader or you feel pretty solid about the draft in hand, you might want to invite the reader to give whatever kind of feedback he or she most wants to give. And sometimes a writer will invite you to give whatever feedback you want. In such a situation it's helpful to realize that you can select among the kinds of feedback and give a kind of blend. We will end with an example of such a blending for each of the essays we've been dealing with.

We put this blend in the form of a letter since that's the form we use most often for giving feedback to our friends, colleagues, and students. And it's the form we usually ask our students to use with each other. The letter is a friendly and flexible form.

Dear Yoko,

I was impressed by your essay but it made me struggle too. I learned a lot from it and it made me think—think hard—but as I was reading I often wanted to argue against you. Now that I've read your essay a couple of times and thought about it, I don't resist you so much, but I still resist some. I don't feel as though I'm finished reacting and digesting your essay. Here are some responses at this point.

*Final Word:
Taking Charge
of the Feedback
Process
by Choosing
among These
Techniques*

47

As I read your essay, I hear you arguing for the importance and value of Black English, arguing that it should be used and taught, and criticizing people who want to prevent that from happening.

Up till now, I've always considered Ebonics a type of slang; I've always been taught that it is simply "loose" or "bad" English—that the places where it differs from Standard English are "mistakes." But now you are making me think again. Is it a real language that follows a full set of rules? If so, I need to rethink my resistance, especially since my experience has come as a white person brought up in white neighborhoods and schools.

Despite any resistance, I had no trouble seeing lots of strong points in your essay. You'll see on your paper where I've put straight lines underneath words and phrases or alongside passages that I felt as especially strong or clear or striking. I used some wiggly lines at points where something didn't work so well for me.

Here are other strengths I felt:

It's clear, strong, sincere writing throughout. Impassioned but not shouting.

You come at this issue from an outside angle. It's powerful to open with an image of kids in Japan and close by talking about the U.S. being valued by others for its diversity.

I guess it's your outside point of view that helps you sidestep the either/or fight and stand up for both sides of the argument. That is, even though you are arguing for teaching Black English and inviting it to be used, still you are also saying that black children should be taught to be good at using Standard English. But maybe you could make this approach even clearer. For throughout my first reading, I thought you were only on the Black English side of the fight. I didn't quite figure out your middle position or double position till my second reading.

Here are some of the questions I had as I was reading:

Can you say more about how society is hurting children's identity by not teaching Ebonics in schools? I agree with you that "children have the right to their own language," but can't they speak their language at home, with friends, and in the neighborhood? Will the language die if it isn't taught in class? Or do you think it will?

Can you explain what you mean when you say, "When the bilingually educated blacks consist of the majority of the Black population of America, it will again change the white people's ways of thinking and the history of this country."

Can you pay a bit more attention to arguments against bilingual education? This would have been helpful for me and might have helped other resistant readers.

Thanks for making me think so hard and making me open up an issue I thought was closed.

• • •

Dear Gabrielle,

It was a treat to read your essay. I never would have thought of fulfilling an essay assignment by writing something like this. I don't even know what to call it. My overall feeling is that *you* could get away with it, but *I* never could. But maybe your example will make me try to experiment. But I have a feeling I never could do it like you do.

I drew straight lines for words and passages that felt strong or hit home. Lots of them. Only one or two wiggly lines where I was confused.

When I started reading your piece, I said to myself, What is going on? But soon it all became very clear. You describe a struggle I often feel. I get sucked right in and it makes me want to read the rest. As I read on and the two voices continue to fight about writing the assignment, I begin to hear the words out loud in my head.

Actually everything about the essay seems strong to me. But I kept thinking about whether the teacher would accept this if the assignment was for an "essay." Really, my main question is, What happened when you turned this in?

I thought the voice that didn't want to write was the strongest, the loudest. It's so true about not being able to write what you want to write for teachers. And yet the other voice was more clever. In a way I was reluctant for that voice to trick the other one into writing. I wanted the other one to hold out and not give in.

As I tried to analyze your piece, my first thought was that it really does the job of an essay because it analyzes so well all the struggles and factors involved in writing for teachers. But then I thought that in a way it's really about something else: how the mind works—how we deal with difficulties. I wondered whether I actually talk to myself this way. I don't think I do. And yet your conversation somehow felt familiar to me.

What seemed particularly clever to me, after thinking about it for a while, was how this essay itself was a kind of example of what it's about. Just like the one part of you has to trick the other part into doing what she doesn't want to do, so this essay has to trick the teacher into accepting something that's different from a regular essay. You are trying to win the teacher over. I like how the essay is about trickery, creativity, and breaking the rules.

Sample Essays

What's Wrong with Black English?

Yoko Koga

"Isn't America a diversified country?" When I learned that there were people who had to abandon their culture and language to be an American, I could not but ask this question. Then I asked, "What does it mean to be an American?" These questions had never come to a Japanese girl whose country consists of only one race and only one language.

Over the past five years or so, many fashionable streets in Tokyo have been flooded with young people wearing big sagging pants and knit caps. It was a fad for a while for girls to braid their hair with beads. They say that the fashion of blacks in the inner cities in America is cool. So they imitate them. Not only the fashion, they also love rap music, reggae, soul music, and Caribbean music. When a famous rap musician came to Budokan, the biggest concert hall in Tokyo, twenty thousand fans rushed to fill it. Every Sunday, Yoyogi Park, the central park of Tokyo, is filled with groups of young people dancing to rap music. They perform so wonderfully that many people stop and watch them. Huge crowds along the street enjoy these performances. Because of the revival of the 60s, films of Martin Luther King, Jr., and Malcolm X were big hits. Blacks of America and their culture have the power of attracting people, especially younger generations.

When I learned that there is a debate among educators whether they should educate black children in Black English or in Standard English, I was surprised. Why should they not educate their children in the children's own language? I thought it was everyone's basic right. Black children should be taught both in Black English (or Ebonics) and Standard English, the language of their own and the language of the country they live in. This bilingual approach helps build poor children's self-esteem immensely. Banning Black English and forcing them to learn Standard English only hurts the children's identity because it means to the children that their language and culture are rejected in the public place. Instead of banning the students' natural English, educators in the black population should teach how powerful Black English and culture are. They should encourage their students by teaching how black culture has influenced American history, has changed people's way of thinking, and attracts people like those in my country, Japan. The insight that originally inspired Lisa D. Delpit to write her seminal article, "Skills and Other Dilemmas" (1987) expresses the point of this issue very well. Although Delpit came to disagree with this formulation later, she stated it succinctly in her 1988 piece, "The Silenced Dialogue":

Children have the right to their own language, their own culture. We must fight cultural hegemony and fight the system by insisting that children be allowed to express themselves in their own language style. It is not they, the children, who must change, but the schools. To push children to do anything else is repressive and reactionary. (280)

I think this statement represents the core idea of bilingual education and any argument should start from the belief that "children have the right to their own language."

There are some people who oppose the idea of bilingual education. They argue that the children whose native languages are not Standard English should be corrected at the beginning of their public education because those languages indicate that one is from the lower class of America, and that jeopardizes children's future success in this society. Richard Rodriguez opposes bilingual education in *Hunger of Memory:*

I have heard "radical" linguists make the point that Black English is a complex and intricate version of English. And I do not doubt it. But neither do I think that Black English should be a language of public instruction. What makes Black English inappropriate in classrooms is not something in the language. It is rather what lower-class speakers make of it. Just as Spanish would have been a dangerous language to use in the schooling of teenagers for whom it reinforces feelings of public separateness. (101)

He claims that speaking the language of lower classes is the cause of public separation. I think, however, the feelings of public separateness do not come from the language only. The feeling arises in minority people, including African Americans, because they cannot be proud of themselves. It is because they know they are economically poor. If you could educate your next generation to be proud of their culture, they could get out of the vicious circle of "uneducated, poor, single mothers depending on welfare." You cannot abandon a language just because it is spoken by poor people. The language is used because there are people who need the language to express their feelings and to hand down their culture to the next generation. In a way, a language is a culture. Destroying a language is destroying people, because if you lose your language, you lose the way of expressing yourself. When the bilingually educated blacks consist of the majority of the black population of America, it will again change the white people's ways of thinking and the history of this country.

The argument that teaching Standard English to black children is important is understandable since Standard English and an understanding of white middle class rules and codes are necessary tools for social success. Children from the poor area should be taught these rules because, like it or not, they mark the place where "power" currently exists, and the children must get into there eventually. However, the children's own "English" should still be the public language in the classroom. Ideally the students should be taught by "bilingual" teachers who speak and understand the values and problems of both cultures, white middle class and black. As Delpit suggested in "The Silenced Dialogue":

Appropriate education for poor children and children of color can only be devised in consultation with adults who share their culture. Black parents, teachers of color, and members of poor communities must be allowed to participate fully in the discussion of what kind of instruction is in their children's best interest. Good liberal intentions are not enough. (282)

The advocates of nonbilingual education may believe that the only culture in this country should be the one of the dominant white middle class. Hence everybody should speak "their" English, the so-called Standard English. However, the cultures of America which people of other countries admire are not only the whites'. When many Japanese say they love America, they mention the "cultures" of America. The reason people love America is its diversity. And they are amazed at the generosity this country shows to its diverse population. America's capacity for holding so many different people and cultures has been one of the major attractions that draws so many people to this country. In the nineteenth century, many people came to the New World because they saw this country as a melting pot of many ethnic groups, and they thought there would be a room for them to live their lives. I think this is still the main reason for people coming to this country. If America starts denying its diversity by unifying its languages, it means it denies its history and the spirit of the country. To hold the richness of its culture, America should keep education its next generation in various languages. Coming from the racially homogeneous country like Japan, I see the standardization of America as a great loss to today's diversified world.

Works Cited

Delpit, Lisa D. "The Silenced Dialogue: Power and Pedagogy in Educating Other People's Children." *Harvard Educational Review* 58.3 (1988): 280–98.
Rodriguez, Richard. *Hunger of Memory: The Education of Richard Rodriguez.* Boston: D. R. Godine, 1982.

The Power of Sprinkles

Gabrielle Radik

"I don't want to do this! I'm bored, and I'm tired, and this thing doesn't make any sense, and everyone's watching the movie in the other room, and I want to watch too, and I don't want to do this I don't want to do this I don't want to do this!"

"We have to do this. It's important. If we don't turn in the essays then we don't do well in the class and we won't be able to participate in the discussion and our grade will go down and our GPA will suffer and we'll lose some of our scholarships."

"But you know I hate writing! Especially this kind, because we have to say things the way the teacher wants to hear them, and as often as not we have to do research and work it into the paper somewhere. Sometimes they make us argue a point, and I just don't like doing that."

"You're arguing a point right now. You argue all the time. And we've done writing before—we write to make lists, and give directions. Every now and again we take notes."

"When was the last time we took notes, I'd like to know? If we've taken notes recently, then I had nothing to do with it!"

"OK, never mind about the notes. Forget the notes. We write memos to the roommate, and we write stupid messages on the door."

"Yeah . . . but . . . but those don't take very long, and if we don't write the lists, then we forget things. And if we don't write directions, then no one can find us. And if we don't write the memos, then the roommate gets annoyed. And stupid messages aren't just stupid—they're fun!"

"We write e-mail. That takes a long time. We spend time every day writing e-mail."

"E-mail isn't the same! The messages are fun, like all those forwards we send. Besides, we're in a contest with the friend about how many e-mail forwards we can send each other! You know that! And when we write to the other friends it's because we can't talk to them because the phone is too expensive. You know I like people."

"Sometimes it isn't e-mail though. We've written letters to the friends. Those are always long. And what about the diary?"

"We only write to the friends when we can't talk to them or when there's a problem and we want them to listen to everything we have to say. And how often do we add to the diary? I'll tell you when. Only when we have stuff to argue about or when we've done something we don't want to forget. It only has five entries. It doesn't count."

"Well, if you can write for that, why can't you write for this?"

"Because this is assigned! It's something we were told we had to do; there's a certain way that we're supposed to do it. If we do it my way, it doesn't count. We have to finish it by a certain time, and anything I have to do by a certain time isn't fun. It's duty. And we have to make it a certain length; I can't just say what I want to say. We have to make sure we're saying enough or it'll look like we didn't put any work into it because it isn't long enough."

"Sometimes a minimum length is good. It tells us how much detail we're supposed to go into and how much we should say about something."

"Yeah, well, sort of. But then there's what happens when we've finished everything we want to say and we think it's good and it makes sense the way we have it and adding more would make it worse. But it isn't long enough! If we pass it in the way it is, we get marked down because we didn't do enough work. So we have to add stuff somewhere in the end, or somewhere in the thing, that really isn't important, just to make it longer. It's hard putting in bull_ _ _ _ without making it look like bull_ _ _ _. Or when we come to as long as it's supposed to be, and we still have more to say."

"All right, you have a point there. But the teacher-person has to penalize students for that sort of thing, or the stupid people would get away with too much."

"Yeah, I suppose."

"We've been writing them for years. Book reports, essays, research papers, thesis papers, lots of stuff."

"And I hated every minute of them. Remember, I put up a fight every time."

"You mean you whined every time."

"Hey! It's only because we never do things my way."

"We don't always have to do things the way we're supposed to. Sometimes it works much better if we do our own thing, and just make it look like what it's supposed to be. We've written those Green Eggs & Ham things. Those were sort of like essays. You enjoyed those."

"We didn't have to make those look like anything. They were just because we wanted to, and they were silly and random. I like random silly stuff. Like tapeworms and pickles and plungers and iguanas and anything beginning with J and . . ."

"OK, OK, I get the picture. How about we just do this assignment, and then we can go watch the movie. I want to see it, too, you know. We'll just make this one random somehow. Yeah, we'll put in something silly, just as long as the whole thing makes sense so that the teacher-person is happy. And as soon as it's over, we can get a Smurf sundae . . ."

"With sprinkles?"

"Of course."

"It's a deal. Let's get started . . ."